The Lewis Land Struggle

Na Gaisgich

acair

The publishers extend their appreciation to Cuimhneachain nan Gaisgeach for
permission to publish this book.

The publishers acknowledge subsidy from the Scottish Arts Council towards
the publication of this volume.

The publishers are also grateful for asistance from
the West Highland Free Press, Skye.

Permission to reproduce the illustrations by courtesy of:
Scottish Record Office AF 67/38
The Illustrated London News Picture Library
Lewis Museum Trust
Stornoway Library
Mitchell Library, Glasgow City Libraries (*The Bulletin*)
Comann Eachdraidh Bheàrnaraigh
British Library (*The Graphic*, January 7th, 1888 and
the *North British Daily Mail*, November, 1887)
"By Courtesy of Edinburgh City Libraries" (*Secretary for Scotland:
A sketch of the High Office and the Statesmen who have been
Scottish Secretaries 1885-1918*)
Eòlas
Derick Mackenzie
The Trustees of the National Library of Scotland

Private Collections:
Will Maclean	Miss Jean Macdonald
Deirdre Macdonald	George Macdonald
Andrew MacMorrine	Cree Mackenzie
Duncan Morison	Angus Macleod
Mary Ann Mackinnon	John Mackay
William Macaulay	Henrietta Smith
George Stewart	Donald Maclean

Permission to reproduce texts from *Oighreachd agus Gabhaltas*:
Department of Celtic Studies, University of Aberdeen;
An t-Ollamh Dòmhnall MacAmhlaigh; Iain M MacLeòid; Iain MacArtair

Cover photography Eòlas

ISBN 0 86152 166 8

© Acair

First published in Scotland in 1996 by Acair Ltd.,
7 James Street, Stornoway, Isle of Lewis.

This first reprinting by Acair in 1998

All rights reserved. No part of this publication may be reproduced
without the prior permission of the publisher.

Design by Acair
Printed by the Stornoway Gazette

Contents

	Pg.
Foreword	5
Angus Macleod	
Introduction	7
Notes and References	22
1 Bernera	25
Notes and References	37
2 The Park Deer Raid	39
The Raid	48
The Military and the Arrests	54
The Trial	59
The Aftermath	65
Notes and References	68
3 Aignish 1888: The Struggle Intensifies	70
The Background	78
The Trial	81
The Months After the Trial	87
Notes and References	91
4 Coll and Gress	93
The Raiders, Lord Leverhulme and the Board, 1920	106
The Final Years	118
Notes and References	128
5 The Wider Struggle	132
Notes and References	135

6 Selected Songs and Poems 136

    Oran air Bill nan Croitearan 136
    Song about the Crofters' Bill 137

    Croitearan Leòdhais 138
    The Lewis Crofters 140

    Oran Muinntir Bheàrnaraigh 142
    Song to the People of Bernera 145

    Ceatharnaich Bheàrnaraigh 148
    The Heroes of Bernera 150

    Ruaig an Fhèidh 152
    The Deer Drive 154

    Spiorad a' Charthannais 156
    The Spirit of Kindliness 164

Ro-Radh 177
    Aonghas MacLeòid

7 Gaisgich Bheàrnaraigh 1874 179
    An t-Ollamh Dòmhnall MacAmhlaigh

8 Reud na Pairce 1887 188
    Iain M MacLeòid

9 Aimhreit Aignis 1888 198
    Iain MacArtair

10 Col Uarach agus Griais 206
    Seòras Stiùbhart

Foreword

Cuimhneachain nan Gaisgeach was founded in 1989 to commemorate our forebears' struggles for land law reform. We wanted to generate awareness of local history and how precious rights, which today are taken for granted, were won by their efforts.

It was resolved to commemorate four main events in the Lewis land struggle by erecting the very best memorials we could possibly achieve. So far, three of these have been magnificently designed by the acclaimed artist, Will MacLean, and constructed with equal skill by James Crawford.

Cuimhneachain nan Gaisgeach also invited Joni Buchanan of Uig, Lewis, who has written extensively on the land issue, to describe for posterity these four crucial episodes in the history of our island and of the wider struggle for the land. This book is the result and her splendid text is supported by brief accounts in Gaelic by distinguished local authors, as well as contemporary poetry relating to the issues of land ownership and rights. We are grateful to Professor Donald Meek of Aberdeen University for his researches, and Ian MacDonald of the Gaelic Books Council for his assistance with translation.

The Lewis Land Struggle will focus the attention of this and future generations on the struggles which our forebears had to endure in order to emancipate themselves and us from the thraldom imposed by heartless and rapacious landlords. It will also be valued by students who in future may research this period in Lewis history.

Cuimhneachain nan Gaisgeach has further plans to commemorate these great people and events, including an interpretative centre, possibly to be incorporated into the proposed Lochs Community School. This would portray the history of crofting life and the struggles for land reform which have allowed crofting to survive down to the present day.

This book includes a wealth of new information and, unlike many histories of the Highlands and Islands, is written from a perspective which is sympathetic to the crofters and their desperate need for land. If these four battles, and others like them, had not been fought and won, Lewis today would be as barren of people as are so many other parts of the Highlands and Islands. We owe so much to Na Gaisgich -The Land Heroes.

Angus Macleod MBE

Stornoway, 1852.

Introduction

"Mr James Matheson took an active part in the importation of the drug and did not permit either the foolish regulations of the Chinese Custom House or the horrors of actual war to deter him from faithfully carrying out his self-imposed task; and after aiding in the glorious work of regenerating China and awakening the poor heathens to the advantages of opium, he returned to his native land the possessor of an ample fortune, nobly and honourably won."

Glasgow News, June 27th, 1887.

"I am certain that the people are more frightened of the proprietor and the factor than they are of the God who created them."

Alexander Morrison, merchant and Chairman of the Stornoway branch of the Highland Land Law Reform Association, in his evidence to the Napier Commission, 1883.

This account of land agitation on the Island of Lewis in the period 1874-1922 focuses on four case studies. In chronological order, there was the conflict which has passed into history as the Bernera Riot, and proved seminal in encouraging others to believe that the capricious power of landlordism could be successfully resisted; the raid on the Park Deer Forest on the east of the island, which challenged the whole ethos of "deer before men"; the Aignish confrontation, which highlighted the conflict between large farms and the claims of the landless in search of small-holdings; and finally a momentous struggle of wills which was concentrated on the farms of Coll and Gress in the district of Back, after the First World War. In each case crofter demonstrations against the estate led directly or indirectly to the acquisition of more land for crofting.

Through generations, the Earls of Seaforth had been the feudal Lords of Lewis. On his death in 1815, Lord Seaforth was succeeded by his eldest daughter, Mrs Stewart MacKenzie of Seaforth. The estate had been entailed following the Jacobite rebellions and had fallen into heavy and prolonged debt. (1) The island's economy had long been sustained by the domestic fishing, cattle, kelp and to some extent illicit distilling. (2) In the early decades of the 19th century, a decline in the price of cattle combined with the fall in demand for kelp to create poor economic conditions for the crofters. This had an adverse effect on the Seaforth fortunes; when they could no longer rely on rent to sustain them they turned their attention to big sheep farming as the most lucrative source of income. (3)

The interiors of the hilly parishes of Uig in the south-west and Park in the east were put under sheep during the first three decades of the 19th century and the people, for the most part, cleared to Canada. (4) All of the farms which were subsequently raided had been cleared by the Seaforths, who had long since divested themselves of any notion of clan-based or feudal responsibility. When Mr Stewart MacKenzie was appointed Governor of the Ionian Islands and later of Ceylon the island was managed by Edinburgh-based agents. During that period there was no estate expenditure on the island; the sole function of the agents was to collect rents.

Towards the end of the Seaforth era the Lewis economy was moving inexorably towards crisis and the people increasingly unable to meet the demands for rent. In 1835-36 poor weather conditions resulted in the failure of the potato crop — which was by then the dominant one — and cattle prices also hit rock bottom. Expecting an upturn in price the following year the crofters used reserve seed and potatoes for animal consumption. Prices remained low and the overall outcome was to throw the people into an unprecedented level of poverty. (5) A period of systematic clearances began in Uig and Park — the 'redundant' population had become too much of a burden on the estate and its absentee proprietors. (6) The introduction of sheep farming brought increased farm rentals, but not enough to relieve the Seaforths of their indebtedness.

By the time the island was sold in 1844, the legacy of the Seaforths' centuries-old proprietorship of Lewis was an impoverished people and a pitifully underdeveloped land. The new proprietor, James Matheson, was a partner in the firm of Jardine Matheson which traded in the Far East. A native of Sutherland, he was born in Lairg in 1796. In 1843 he succeeded his business partner William Jardine as the Whig Member of Parliament for Ashburton and was later both Lord Lieutenant and Member of Parliament for Ross and Cromarty. (7) In 1851, the Baronetcy of Achany was created and the owner of Lewis became Sir James. (8)

Matheson's wealth and influence were firmly rooted in the opium trade. He had progressed from employment in Calcutta with his uncle's firm, MacIntosh and Co., to Canton in the 1820s where he became a major business figure in his own right. (9) In 1832, he joined forces with William Jardine to form Jardine Matheson, which developed enormous interests in banking, insurance and shipping. They traded in tea, silk and cotton but cash from the sale and transportation of the opium underpinned all of the company's trade. James Matheson wrote in 1833: "The command of money which we derive from our large opium dealings and which can hardly be derived from any other source gives us an important advantage." (10)

The Chinese, determined to put an end to the devastating social and physical effects of opium addiction and to halt the outflow of silver, had banned the drug and issued edicts against its importation, but James Matheson regarded these as "so much waste paper." (11) His nephew Donald Matheson took a moral stance and resigned from the firm because of its connections with the drug trade. But James Matheson

Sir James Matheson. A native of Sutherland, he made his fortune in the East, trading in tea, silk and opium.

declared that he had "never seen a native in the least bestialised by opium smoking." The part played by the firm in the subsequent 'Opium Wars' led Disraeli to describe Matheson as "a dreadful man, richer than Croesus, one McDrug, fresh from Canton with a million of opium in each pocket." (12) When Matheson returned to Britain, his business interests were focused on the UK arm of Jardine Matheson at Lombard Street in London — and increasingly on the Isle of Lewis.

There are many conflicting accounts of Sir James Matheson's proprietorship of Lewis, especially in relation to the capital which he invested in the island. (13) On the whole, history has treated him with extraordinary generosity. Certainly, Matheson used his shipping connections well and greatly improved communications to and from the island. (14) However the greater part of capital spent on infrastructure — schools, roads, curing houses and other improvements — was recouped in the form of tax or rent. (15) There was little spent on crofter dwellings or on improving crofters' land. (16) Capital was invested on specific projects — such as the reclamation of farm land and on estate buildings and steadings — which had little direct relevance to the crofting population.

Recent histories of the Clearances have also treated Matheson kindly, but a closer look at his proprietorship of Lewis raises more questions than can be adequately addressed in this account. Suffice to say that he may have been marginally more benevolent than the worst of the Highland landlords, as he could well afford to be, but ultimately chose to go down the same road of eviction and emigration. (17)

The more sympathetic portrayal of Matheson is largely attributable to the emphasis placed on his apparent efforts to mitigate the impact of the potato famine which had recurred in the mid 1840s bringing years of misery throughout the Highlands and Islands. In general, landlords' response to the widespread destitution was eviction and emigration, on an unprecedented level even in Highland terms. On Lewis, during the first few years of his proprietorship Matheson instigated 'work-schemes' as an alternative to emigration. It was a response which singled him out and staved off emigration for about four years. However the schemes were as exploitative as they were compassionate; instead of helping people on the edge of starvation the schemes served the estate's purpose well by using a substantial pool of labour to effect estate improvements at minimal cost. (18)

During the potato famine, large quantities of meal were supplied to Highland estates at government expense. In Lewis, the estate distributed the relief meal only in exchange for labour on Matheson's work-schemes. (19) Similarly, seed potatoes supplied by southern charities were sold at 25% of the market value — and if the tenant could not meet the cost of the potatoes or the relief meal it was added on as another item of rent under the heading "balance of destitution meal." (20)

Where crofting land was drained the rents were raised. Road tax was added to the crofters' rent where township roads were constructed. And, invariably, the meagre wages paid by the estate had conditions attached — one-third was to go on payment

Sir James Matheson and his nephew, Donald Matheson, who resigned from his uncle's firm because of its connection with the opium trade.

of rent, and if the labourer was in arrears of rent a portion of the wage was kept in lieu of payment. (21) In an impoverished community, where rent arrears and other debts were endemic, the schemes were seen as yet another instrument of repression, and offered no possibility of improving the crofters' lot.

The township of Reef in West Uig was one of the first to be cleared by Matheson. John Scobie, his first factor, issued the tenantry with eviction notices in 1848-49. The villagers, over 30 families, disregarded the removal notices and refused to go. Their strong defiance against the estate was, at that time, almost certainly unprecedented in Lewis, although crofters in Harris and North Uist had resisted evictions in the preceding years. The people of Reef held on to their lands and homes for three years before they were finally moved by John Munro MacKenzie, Matheson's second factor. He broke their spirit and forced them into arrears by preventing the people of Reef from obtaining employment during the famine years on the landlord's 'work-schemes' in Uig.

"So when they turned out in this way and refused to leave the place, each foreman having little charge of the works got notice that no work was to be given to the people of this place. They then fell into arrears of rent ... and so when this additional hold was got on them, go they must, because the rent was not paid," recalled a former villager who gave evidence to the Napier Commission. (22)

The work-schemes soon gave way to emigration, sponsored by the Matheson estate. Once again, most historical accounts have treated Matheson kindly by suggesting there was no forced emigration from Lewis. Examination of primary sources, and particularly John Munro Mackenzie's 1851 diary, confirms that this was far from the truth, as the factor spells out the daily organisation of emigrants. (23) In the Napier Commission evidence, crofters repeatedly rejected both the assumption that Matheson's schemes were ever designed to alleviate want, and the notion that the 1851 emigrations were conducted with the consent of the population.

After the clearances and dispossessions of the 1850s, the relative economic stability of the next two decades should have led to an improvement in the local economy. Agricultural prices were good and although big sheep farmers were the principal beneficiaries, the general buoyancy did filter through to the crofting class. The seasonal outflow of workers by the 1860s went beyond Caithness and east coast ports as the young men and women from the islands sought employment as agricultural workers on lowland farms. Later on, the women and girls went into domestic service in the cities. All of these forms of employment away from Lewis led to cash being returned to homes on the island.

But it was a fragile improvement, and the ability of the islanders to keep body and soul together was still largely at the mercy of the landowner, the burdens he imposed and the regime over which he presided. That the Bernera Riot took place in 1874, as a reaction against over-bearing conditions of life, suggests that Lewis remained largely in an economic and social time-warp during these first 30 years of

Matheson's proprietorship. When the Napier Commission collected its evidence about the preamble to that explosion of feeling, almost every witness described the acute poverty of the people. The crofters had been maintained as an economically powerless class, hopelessly unable to accumulate capital even in the years of some prosperity and stability. In those years their modest surpluses went towards rent, other estate-imposed burdens and provisions.

John Munro MacKenzie had resigned as Chamberlain in 1853 and was succeeded by Donald Munro, then a pleader in Stornoway Sheriff Court and the island's Procurator Fiscal. Munro was an odious man. In a contemporary account of life on the Matheson estate, Daniel MacKinlay wrote: "He (Munro) had so wormed himself into the confidence of the proprietor, that he was allowed to manage the people and the estate without any control; and he ruled over them with a rod of iron. The crofter tenants-at-will were quite at his mercy and nothing was done to improve their lot." (25)

Munro was a tyrant, but he was also Sir James Matheson's favourite factor, so he remained in that position for 25 years. He also held another 15 posts concurrently, including Procurator Fiscal, Baron Baillie, Commanding Officer of the Volunteer Force and chairman of all the Parochial Boards and Boards of Education. (26) Even the deeply discrediting events which led to the Bernera Riot did not make Matheson get rid of his favourite factor. Immediately after the trial which resulted, Matheson proclaimed he would stick by Munro "as long as he lived." In fact Munro was removed from his various posts shortly afterwards. The apologia about "landlord not knowing what his factor was doing" holds no water in the relationship between Matheson and Munro.

The fact that Lewis crofters remained 'tenants-at-will' throughout the period of recovery and until the passing of the first Crofting Act in 1886, was indicative of poor estate management and a considerable obstacle to improvement. The land was held on a presumed verbal lease, commonly of one year's duration. Their status could command no redress in law and subjected the class to the absolute and arbitrary power of the landlord. Security of tenure for a period of 5-6 years could only be granted if certain conditions were met. These included the building of a suitable house; the payment of all arrears of rent; and enough capital to stock the land. Munro MacKenzie said in his evidence to the Napier Commission that "these leases were not much asked for by the tenants ... as they were too slow in doing their part." As the Bernera case, and indeed every other eviction shows, the estate was not slow to capitalise on the crofters' lack of formal rights.

There was no question of compensation for improvements either to the land or to the dwelling. Writing in 1878, MacKinlay condemned the estate's failure to issue long leases and quoted the observations of a Mr Smith who was the tenant of Galson Farm: "Without a lease the crofter has no inducement to improve or drain his land, as his doing so would only tend to a raise in his rent; and being merely a tenant-at-will he is simply dependent on the factor or the ground officer for a roof to cover himself and his family.

"At the present moment you will find families, crowded together, living off the produce of one lot; and but for the sea-fishing at home and the herring fishing on the east coast, combined with the liberality of some of their neighbours in giving them patches of land, they would certainly starve. On the whole the effect is demoralising, and the poor people seem to have fallen into something like a state of indifference as to what their future may be." (27)

Mr Napier Campbell, a Stornoway solicitor, in his evidence to the Napier Commission deplored the absence of legal protection for the crofters and declared that he could only "counsel instant submission lest the worst could come of it ... it is not for themselves alone that crofters are concerned but for their parents, grandparents, wives and children." He added that it would take "great independence, some means, considerable nerve and resolute steadfastness of purpose" to obtain justice from the legal system in Lewis.

The turning point for the crofting population finally came in 1874 when the Bernera crofters challenged the immense and arbitrary power of the Matheson estate. The trial of the Bernera men became a cause célèbre and drew widespread attention to the subjugation of the Lewis crofters. In spite of Matheson's loyalty to Munro, it did lead to the hated factor's resignation and his removal from the many public offices which he also held. Of even greater significance was the tremendous psychological boost which permeated the crofting community after the trial. The Bernera crofters had successfully challenged Munro, evictions were cancelled and they retained the grazing land which was at the centre of the dispute. Their more militant stance was hailed by radical opinion throughout the country, and their success cleared the way for others to take a hand in shaping their own destiny.

Further discontent was muted while the bulk of crofters were able to earn ancillary income to supplement their dwindling agricultural returns. However, in the early 1880s, the period of relative stability came to an end. Agricultural prices reached an all-time low, and the fishing failed. For two successive seasons, hundreds returned from the east coast penniless. Bad weather ruined the crops in 1882-83 and, for the same reason, domestic fishing was more or less abandoned. (28) Things were worse for the landless cottars than for the crofters. Without land, they were more or less dependent on ancillary income and when these sources, particularly the fishing, dried up they had nothing to fall back on.

This new crisis of the early 1880s demonstrated the insecurity of the base on which recovery had been temporarily founded. Preoccupied with events in Ireland, Parliament continued to resist calls for state intervention in Highland affairs until eventually they were left with little choice.

The crucial initiative came from the Braes crofters in Skye, who were the first to adopt the tactic of the Irish Land League by refusing to pay rent and resisting evictions.

Lady Matheson, proprietrix from 1878. No friend of the crofter population, Lady Matheson once told a delegation of crofters petitioning for more land: "The land under sheep and deer is my property and I can do with it what I like."

According to a confidential report to the Secretary of State for Scotland on the rise of crofter agitation, the return of fishermen from Kinsale immediately preceded the first notice of discontent in Braes. These were followed by the visit of an Irish 'emissary', a Mr McHugh. The report noted: "His presence was succeeded by the lawless outbreak in Glendale; publications of a socialist tendency were, and still are, widely circulated among the population through agencies in London; cartoons showing mitred ecclesiastics crushing a snake marked 'Landlordism' were distributed." (29)

In Lewis, Lady Matheson had taken over as proprietrix on the death of her husband in the south of France in 1878. Though the outcome of the Bernera case had exposed the bullying regime which the estate operated, and led to some toning down of its practices, Lewis continued to be run with the same high-handed insensitivity. The emphasis continued to be on extending tenanted farms and deer forests with a complete disregard for the consequences which flowed from this usurpation of land for the crofting majority and the even more impoverished landless cottars. At long last, however, there was a political vehicle through which to contest such grievances.

The proliferation of crofter agitation, rent strikes and land seizures which followed the Battle of the Braes in April 1882 aroused national, and indeed international interest and helped create a tide of radical opinion in favour of the crofters' cause. This was given political expression by the emergence of a pro-crofter coalition which took the name of the Highland Land Law Reform Association and later became the Highland Land League.

In February 1883, a Home Office report concluded that "there is so much discontent amongst West Highland and Island crofters" that the Government should intervene in crofting affairs for the first time since the distribution of relief meal during the famine years 40 years earlier. It was this recommendation and the persistence of a group of pro-crofter MPs already in the House of Commons which led to the establishment of the Royal Commission on the Highlands and Islands under the chairmanship of Lord Napier of Ettrick. The commission was to inquire into the conditions of the crofting population in the Highlands and Islands of Scotland.

The Land League, all over the Highlands and Islands, began to organise demonstrations and meetings to help crofters articulate their grievances when the commission took evidence in each area. In Lewis, the League had established an effective branch structure. The same government report which pronounced on the sources of land agitation in Braes noted that "all cottars, squatters, and the young men in Lewis, especially those in the Royal Naval Reserve, are members of the League." (30) The most prominent figure to publicly emerge in connection with the League was Rev. Angus MacIver, minister of the Church of Scotland in Uig.

The Uig committee met in Valtos Glen early in 1883 and resolved to organise a large demonstration before the Napier Commission's visit to the island. In March over 2,000 people, from every corner of the island, made their way to Stornoway and

The last Matheson to own Lewis, Major Duncan, who sold to Lord Leverhulme.

Dr. G. B. Clark

Charles Fraser-MacIntosh

D. H. MacFarlane

Dr. R. MacDonald

John Cameron

The 'Crofter MPs' who were elected in 1885 under the banner of the Highland Land Law Reform Association.

gathered in Perceval Square. As usual, then and now, the meeting was opened with prayer. Rev. Angus MacIver presided and was supported by a further 20 speakers including Murdo MacLean, fishcurer, Valtos, Roderick MacLeod, Bayble, Alexander Morrison, chairman of the Stornoway branch and John MacAulay, Valtos. Angus MacIver, reported the *The Oban Times*, "entered fully into the various phases of the land question and the many grievances the crofters laboured under. Signatures were then gathered for a petition which was to be sent to the Prime Minister." (31)

All the famous names connected with the land reform movement visited Lewis during these vital years of agitation — John MacPherson, the Glendale Martyr; John Murdoch, editor of *The Highlander*; Donald MacCallum, Waternish; and the great friend of the crofters in Parliament prior to their own MPs being elected, Donald Horne MacFarlane, a Caithness man who represented County Carlow. (32) John MacPherson and Donald MacCallum joined a Land League demonstration in Stornoway in November 1884. "All the town was alive with people," reported the *The Oban Times*, "...they formed a procession of 1,400 people, with banners of all descriptions with mottoes in Gaelic and English floating gaily above their heads." Just a few years earlier, such an open show of hostility to the estate would have been inconceivable, but the mood had turned and the purpose of that gathering was to organise support for the crofter candidates at the forthcoming election.

The new 'crofter MPs' were an extraordinary group of men. Donald MacFarlane, who had previously been the Parnellite MP for County Carlow and had championed the crofters' cause in the House of Commons, won a famous victory in Argyll. Charles Fraser-MacIntosh — a member of the Napier Commission who was despised by the landlords as "one of their own kind" who had turned coat — triumphed in Inverness-shire. Dr. Gavin Clark, an advocate of land nationalisation and consul for the Boers in London, won Caithness without the benefit of previous connections there. The Northern Burghs seat was taken by John Cameron, a Gaelic-speaking industrial chemist. Lewis itself contributed to the success in Ross and Cromarty of Dr. Roderick MacDonald, a London-based champion of the Highland Land Law Reform Association and the crofters' cause. Only Angus Sutherland in the county of Sutherland was defeated by "the Radical Marquis" of Stafford, who stood on his own platform of Land Reform, but Sutherland took the seat in the election of the following year. Their success represented an astonishing upheaval in Highland politics and an irresistible symbol of the demand for crofters' rights.

The verbatim volumes of evidence given to the Napier Commission, as it made its way round the Highlands and Islands, represents the most powerful surviving testimony to the realities of 19th century history as perceived by the people who lived through these decades of poverty and oppression — not least on Lewis, under the Seaforths and then the Mathesons. The findings of the Commission, allied to the electoral success of HLLRA candidates, led directly to the crucial Crofters Act of 1886, establishing security of tenure and greatly constraining the power of landlords.

Lord Leverhulme, a strong minded proprietor, whose hostility to crofting led to one of the most troubled periods in the island's history.

While the very existence of a crofting population in many parts of Lewis was only sustained because of the 1886 legislation, it did not go nearly far enough for the balance of history to be redressed. In particular, it did not return to crofting hands most of the great acreages which had been taken away in previous decades for sheep and deer. In other words, it consolidated the population where it still existed, but by and large did not address the wider issue of land from which crofters and their stock had already been successfully excluded. In many parts of the Highlands and Islands, that distinction survives down to the present day. In others, it was removed in succeeding decades through the extension of the area under crofting tenure.

The Park Deer Raid and the Aignish Conflict were two outstanding illustrations of the frustration and deprivation which continued to be felt in the period immediately after the passing into law of the 1886 Act. In Park the source of grievance was the huge hinterland of the crofting villages which was still rented by the Matheson estate to a sporting tenant for the pursuit of deer. In Aignish, the clash of interests was between a large agricultural tenant, who farmed the land which the local people desperately needed in order to gain access to the means of livelihood. In each case the British military was deployed to deal with the threat of crofter insurrection.

Essentially the same grievances persisted into the 20th century. The local population, poor and over-crowded, coveted the land which they believed to be rightfully theirs. Far from drawing a line under this period, the end of the First World War accentuated the source of grievance. By this time, Lewis had passed out of Matheson hands and had been acquired by Lord Leverhulme, founder of the enormous soap and fisheries empire which survives down to the present day. His arrival on Lewis and subsequent ambitions for the creation of a Port Sunlight in the Hebrides gave rise to a classic conflict of interests — particularly over the occupation of farmland, which Leverhulme wanted for the supply of milk to his envisaged industrial hub in Stornoway, while landless ex-servicemen were determined to have it for their homes and crofts. Once again, history has tended to treat Leverhulme more kindly than the crofters. This account of events may help to redress the balance.

The primary purpose of this book is to tell the story of four struggles, each of which was crucial in ensuring that the Island of Lewis should continue to have a substantial indigenous population, with rights to remain on the land as crofters. Without these struggles — and others like them — it is certain that many of the places on Lewis in which the Gaelic language and the laughter of children are still heard would not exist as living communities. They deserve to be honoured. The men and women who challenged the power of landlordism, with historic consequences, should be remembered with gratitude on their own island.

Joni Buchanan
July, 1996

Notes and References

1. Donald Macdonald, *Lewis: A History of the Island*, Edinburgh, 1978.

2. James Hunter, *The Making of the Crofting Community*, Edinburgh, 1976. M. Gray, *The Highland Economy*, Edinburgh, 1957. Old Statistical Account, Edinburgh, 1797. New Statistical Account, Edinburgh, 1835-45.

3. Seaforth Papers, GD 46, Scottish Records Office. Donald Macdonald, *Lewis: A History of the Island*, Edinburgh, 1978 — the book lists the villages which were cleared during the Seaforth proprietorship. In Uig townships which lay between Gisla and Bernera were cleared and taken over by the landlords in the 1820s when Scalisco, Morsgail and Linshader sheep runs were created; the next decade saw the clearing of all of the villages around the Bay to make way for the farms at Timsgarry, Ardroil and Mealista; throughout the period land was taken out of crofter use to extend sheep runs which later became deer parks. By 1870, 40,000 acres of West Uig were in the hands of seven private tenants. The Seaforths were responsible for the clearing of up to thirty villages in Uig between 1820-40.

4. H.A. Moisley, *Uig: A Hebridean Parish*, Glasgow University, 1962. J.B. Caird, *Park: A Geographical Study of a Lewis Crofting District*, Glasgow, 1958. See also *Royal Commission on the Highlands and Islands,1883, (Napier Commission)* AF 50.

5. Report to the Board of Supervision by Sir John MacNeill on the Western Highlands and Islands, 1851, XXV1.

6. H.A. Moisley, *Uig: A Hebridean Parish*, Glasow University, 1962. J.B. Caird, *Park: A Geographical Study of a Lewis Crofting District*, Glasgow, 1958.

7. M. Keswick, *The Thistle and the Jade: A Celebration of 150 Years of Jardine, Matheson & Co.*, London, 1982, 18-30.

8. J. Munro MacKenzie, *Diary 1851,* Stornoway, 1994. The opening pages of the diary give an account of the preparations for the celebration of James Matheson's baronetcy.

9. M. Keswick, *The Thistle and the Jade: A Celebration of 150 Years of Jardine, Matheson & Co.,* London, 1982, 18-22.

10. Ibid., 55-84.

11. Ibid.

12. B. Disraeli, *Sybil*, London.

13. Donald Macdonald, *Lewis: A History of the Island*, Edinburgh, 1978, 42-43. See also D. MacKinlay, *The Island of Lewis and its Fishermen-Crofters*, London, 1878, XLIV.

14. *Royal Commission on the Highlands and Islands, 1883, (Napier Commission)* AF50. Written evidence of John Scobie, John Munro MacKenzie and William MacKay, factors to the Matheson estate.

15. Ibid.

16. Ibid.

17. Memorial to Sir John Russell of the Poor Law Board of Supervision from Sir James Matheson, contained in the MacNeill Report, 1851.

18. Report to the Board of Supervision by Sir John MacNeill on the Western Highlands and Islands, 1851, XXVI. See also J. Munro MacKenzie, *Diary 1851*, Stornoway, 1994. See also D. MacKinlay, *The Island of Lewis and its Fishermen-Crofters*, London, 1878.

19. D. MacKinlay, *The Island of Lewis and its Fishermen-Crofters*, London, 1878. *Royal Commission on the Highlands and Islands,1883, (Napier Commission)*. J. Munro MacKenzie, *Diary 1851*, Stornoway, 1994. Report to the Board of Supervision by Sir John MacNeill on the Western Highlands and Islands,1851, XXVI.

20. Ibid.

21. Ibid., see J. Munro MacKenzie, *Diary 1851*, Stornoway, 1994.

22. *Royal Commission on the Highlands and Islands, 1883, (Napier Commission)* AF50.

23. J. Munro Mackenzie, *Diary 1851*, Stornoway, 1994. The evictions of 1851 are

detailed in the first months of the factor's diary. Donald Macdonald, *Lewis: A History of the Island,* Edinburgh, 1978, 159-170, lists many of the villages cleared before the Matheson regime.

24. *Royal Commission on the Highlands and Islands, 1883, (Napier Commission)* AF50. Without exception the witnesses to the Commission testify to the poverty of the people of Lewis.

25. D. MacKinlay, *The Island of Lewis and its Fishermen-Crofters*, London, 1878.

26. J. Shaw Grant, *A Shilling For Your Scowl*, Stornoway, 1992.

27. D. MacKinlay, *The Island of Lewis and its Fishermen-Crofters,* London, 1878.

28. J. Hunter, *The Making of the Crofting Community*, Edinburgh, 1976. M. Gray, *The Highland Economy*, Edinburgh, 1957.

29. Confidential report prepared for the Secretary of State for Scotland by Malcolm MacNeil on the Land League in the Highlands. SRO.

30. Ibid.

31. *The Oban Times*, March, 1883.

32. Donald Meek, *D.H. MacFarlane*, Aberdeen, 1995.

1 Bernera

"As Chamberlain he could evict any man from his holding; as Procurator Fiscal he could prosecute any man opposing his authority; as Chief Magistrate and Justice of the Peace he could punish all minor offences in town or country. We know of no other place in the country where the office of Prosecutor and Judge have been delegated to one man."

The Oban Times, September 19th, 1874.

"Had Mr Munro, instead of being Chamberlain of Lews, been an agent in either Connaught or Munster, he would have long ago licked the dust he has for years made the poor men of this island swallow."

Charles Innes, at the trial of the Bernera Rioters, Stornoway, 1874.

In April 1874, 150 crofters from the island of Bernera and other villages in the Parish of Uig marched to Stornoway to take their bitter grievances to the door of the proprietor Sir James Matheson of Achany. Fifty-six families had been served with eviction notices. Two young Bernera men had been arrested. The people, pushed to the edge of their remarkable tolerance, were seeking redress from a proprietor who sought to present himself to the outside world as a benign patrician.

Their brave action in the face of terrible adversity gained little from the proprietor. But the trial that followed led to the downfall of one of the most hated characters in the history of Lewis — Donald Munro, factor to Sir James Matheson from 1853 to 1874 — and cancelled the threats of eviction hanging over tenants. These are the events that have passed into history as the Bernera Riot — undoubtedly a turning-point in the whole saga of Highland landlordism and the responses to it. (1)

The Highland economy was relatively stable during the two decades of Munro's rule, and conditions were such that the crofting population in many areas could improve their lot. (2) However, the crofters of Lewis were never given that opportunity. In 1874 *The Oban Times* reported that the Lewis crofters existed "in a state of virtual slavery... in conditions which in other lands would foster seeds of revolution." (3)

The power of the estate over the crofters' lives was absolute. Munro, the factor, was also the Procurator Fiscal and the chief magistrate. He was chairman of the parochial and school boards; a director of the gas company, the road trust and the harbour trust. He was the town's solicitor, Notary Public, Baron Baillie, a Justice of the Peace and the Commissioner of Supply. (4)

A pamphlet on the Bernera case, published soon after its conclusion in July 1874, described the manner in which Munro exerted his authority: "The poor people complain of their thralldom, and the petty tyrannies to which they are subjected. To give examples — though they will appear almost incredible — if a small tenant enters the official room of the Chamberlain with his head covered, his hands in his pockets, or with apparently unwashed face, he is by that functionary fined; and if offence is given him — though it would appear to be more frequently taken than intended — or if his behests are not at once obeyed with becoming meekness, the poor crofters are invariably threatened with ejection from their lands. Everyone acquainted with the character of the highlander and islander knows the terrifying effect of such a threat. That the Chamberlain has (or had, for it is hoped that it has been withdrawn by this time) the power of carrying his threat into execution, is proved by the proceedings which of late directed public attention to the district." (5)

Donald Munro had the final say in every aspect of people's lives. He evicted them, fined them and treated them with open and utter contempt. He ruled the people of Lewis with a rod of iron for over 20 years, until he was finally brought to account by the crofters of Bernera, aided by the incisive legal mind of Charles Innes, the Inverness solicitor who represented the Bernera men in court. (6)

There had been a long and painful build-up to the event which became known as the Bernera Riot. By most standards, that title suggests a state of insurrection somewhat in excess of the actions which actually transpired. But there is no legal doubt that, Riot or not, the effective resistance shown by the people of Bernera was a landmark in the history of the Highlands and Islands; a challenge to the power of landlordism which encouraged and inspired others to follow.

From time immemorial crofters on the island of Bernera had used grazing land on the West Uig mainland at Beannaibh a' Chuailein which reached out as far Loch Langabhat to graze the cattle in the summer months. (7) In 1872 notice was served by the estate that these grazings were to be added to both the Scaliscro and Morsgail Deer Forests. The crofters were to establish new sheilings at Earshader where they were offered new grazings. A seven mile dyke would have to be built by the crofters to separate the new grazings from the deer shooting, and to avoid the heavy fines imposed on crofters should their animals stray into the forest.

The Bernera crofters did not give up their ancient grazing land lightly. Negotiations went on between them and James MacRae, the ground officer in Uig, through the winter and into spring 1872. In an unprecedented move they insisted on a lease for the new grazings, before agreeing to start the monumental task of building the dyke. The crofters were still at that time tenants-at-will, without any security of tenure. They told the estate that they would continue to use their traditional grazing land until a written document formalising the change and providing them with security was presented to them. MacRae advised them to send a delegation to meet the factor, Munro, in Stornoway. (8)

There the conditions were agreed to. MacRae recounted during the trial: "We came in and saw him. I got the paper I am speaking about from the office of the factor. It was a requisition or petition, or some such document, and was sent to me so that I might get the crofters to sign it. It contained the arrangement under which they agreed to give up the grazings and the summer shielings at Beannaibh a' Chuailein, and take those of Earshader in exchange. I read it to them, and gave it to some of themselves to read. They signed and gave it back to me, and I returned it to the factor's office. There was a good deal of talking between us during the winter and spring of 1871-2 before they signed it..." But while the crofters believed that such a document gave them some security, Munro later made clear that as far as he was concerned their claim to the grazings was to be on the same basis as the one on which they held their crofts — devoid of any security. On this ambiguous basis, the crofters signed and took over the Earshader grazings on Whitsunday 1872. Munro would soon deny the existence, far less the significance, of any such document. (9)

Less than a year later in November 1873 James MacRae was instructed to move the crofters a second time. On Munro's instruction they were to move from Earshader to grazings on the Island of Bernera which had originally belonged to the farm of Hacklete. The issue simmered over the winter, but MacRae was obliged to return to it in March 1874. By this time the crofters, men and women, had completed the dyke which would separate the Earshader grazings from the deer forest. They had delayed the start of the fishing season to finish the dyke and to keep the estate off their backs. The fact that the dyke was completed made little difference to Munro. They were to be removed from Earshader without compensation and without delay. MacRae said: "There was nothing about the dyke in the (estate's) paper, and no word of compensation being paid for it. It was entirely built at the crofters' expense... Some of the people were very indignant at the change proposed... I sympathised with them myself when I remembered the understanding come to with them before they went into Earshader." (10)

The people's indignation was the least of Munro's worries. He told them to remove the cattle from Earshader or else he would bring in the army. "The Volunteers would settle with them," he declared at a meeting in Earshader. Munro had been Commanding Officer of the 1st Company of Ross-shire Artillery Volunteers for many years. At the subsequent trial, Charles Innes commented on the fact that he must be the only law agent in Scotland "to include such an office in the law list." The message was clear — Munro regarded his military connection as a relevant back-up to his unparalleled authority.

However unhappy they were about the latest edict from Munro, it is likely that the crofters would eventually have acceded to it. Indeed they were willing to negotiate

Charles Innes was a partner in the law firm of Charles Fraser-MacIntosh, a Highland Liberal who later became the Crofter MP for Inverness-shire. Innes successfully defended the Bernera rioters.

and may well have accepted the move if the deserted village of Strome had been included in the new deal. (11) However, Munro was impatient. He went ahead with hiring a Sheriff Officer to serve summonses on the 56 crofters involved. Crucially, the summonses did not just refer to the grazings and the crofters' shielings on Earshader. They also covered the houses and crofts of the 56 on Bernera. Each householder was to be evicted from "...houses situated in the several parts of Bernera, together with his share, held in common, of the moor grazings ... and his share of the summer grazings or shieling ground on the farm of Earshader in the Parish of Uig."

Subsequently, in court, Munro would deny that he ever intended to evict the 56 families from their houses and crofts on Bernera. Under cross-examination by Charles Innes, he explained: "I though it right in point of form to include in the summonses the crofts and houses in Bernera." Innes remained sceptical, pointing out that there was nothing in the documents to suggest that the inclusion of the crofts and houses was an insignificant "point of form." Certainly, the people of Bernera — long familiar with Munro's ruthlessness — did not see it that way. Munro confirmed to the court: "I obtained decree on the summonses of removing, and if I so wished it, I could have removed all the tenants from their crofts and houses in Bernera, as well as from their summer grazings in Lewis, because the decrees gave me power to do so." In other words he could do as he pleased, secure in the knowledge that the supposedly liberal proprietor had never questioned his factorial tactics or abuses. On this occasion, he had not told the proprietor what he was doing on the grounds that, "I am not in the habit of consulting Sir James about every little detail connected with the management of the estate." (12)

Innes asked him: "Oh! then you considered the removing of 56 crofters and their families too small a matter to trouble Sir James about?" Munro answered simply: "I did." He did not at this juncture in his evidence deny that there had been an intention to remove the 56 families from anything more than their shielings and grazings. Certainly, the people who watched the Sheriff Officer arriving in Bernera on March 24th, 1874 had no reason to feel confident that the full terms of the summonses would not be implemented.

Munro had hired Colin MacLennan, previously a Sheriff's Officer in Stornoway but then living in Lochalsh, to deliver the summonses. He was accompanied by James MacRae and Peter Bain, exciseman. Around noon, the three men landed opposite the village of Kirkibost. They served the first summonses at Breaclete then went on to Croir and Bosta. In these villages the summonses were accepted in shocked silence. (13)

"The people were very quiet... When they got them I could see they were vexed," said Peter Bain in a masterpiece of under-statement. By early evening the trio had reached Tobson, but news of their grim message had reached the village before them. Peter Bain later reported: "The people there were more angry than the others."

The villagers were required by the Sheriff's Officer's party to gather in the one place. The names of those to be dispossessed were read out, and the notices handed to them. "He called the villagers to wait on him, like vassals attending their liege..." reported *The Oban Times*. (14) The crofters were incandescent with anger, feeling abused, insulted and ashamed of their own powerlessness. Peter Bain said: "I was not surprised at the men getting angry, considering the way in which the ground-officer spoke to them. His language and manner were calculated to provoke their anger." In MacLennan's own evidence to the subsequent court case, he complained that on leaving the village, one of the crowd said: "You should be dragged through the mud and made examples of."

Amidst this escalating hostility, the trio of summons-servers and a constable left Tobson and proceeded across the moor to Valasay. After a while they were pelted from behind with clods of earth, having been followed by a group of angry villagers, young men and women. It was a fairly minor incident but it angered the Sheriff's Officer who was heard to declare: "If I had my rifle I would make some of the Bernera women lament the loss of their sons." MacLennan and his companions abandoned the attempt to serve the three remaining summonses that night and headed for accommodation to a 'safe house' in Hacklete.

After completing their task the next morning, MacLennan and his assistants headed for Loch Riosaidh where they had moored the boat, but they were stopped en route by a band of angry young men enraged at what was happening to the islanders and at MacLennan's threat. The Sheriff's Officer subsequently told the court that one of the young men, Angus MacDonald, had raised the shooting threat with him. "I asked him to let me alone, as I was on my duty, and I also said I was sent by the proprietor. He swore and said what right had I to come from the proprietor or chamberlain, and that they were proprietors of their own land... They then took my water-proof and top-coat and tore them... They jostled and pushed me about and threatened to strip me... They tried to make me swear I would never go back to Bernera to serve summonses, and I promised not to return. I was glad to get away; I was put into a state of fear and alarm by their violent conduct and any person would be the same." (15)

That evening at the Garynahine Inn the Sheriff Officer vowed to get his revenge for these affronts to his authority. MacLennan and Munro between them got up criminal charges of assaulting and injuring an officer of the law against three of the Bernera men — Angus MacDonald, Norman MacAulay and John MacLeod. All three were fishermen. Instead of being summoned to court, in the usual manner, Angus MacDonald (Aonghas Tharmoid — and later known as Aonghas a' Phrìosain) was arrested in Stornoway before receiving any notice of the charges against him.

The fisherman was in Stornoway with two of his work colleagues on April 8th, to collect their share of the fishing income from the Stornoway curers. Without warning he was 'pounced upon' by four over-zealous police constables. Angus MacDonald had been pointed out to the policemen by MacLennan, the Sheriff Officer. The arrest "was more easily resolved upon than done; the policemen found it almost impossible to apprehend the man, and the lookers-on declined to render any assistance," reported *The Highlander*. While Angus MacDonald was held the other two broke free and hid at the town's curing houses.

The police lured Angus into a close in the centre of town and four policemen tried to hold him down. The fisherman managed, however, to break free and raced up Francis Street with the policemen at his heels. One of the constables managed to undo MacDonald's braces, his trousers fell down and tripped him up. A Valtos baker, John Smith, tried to help Angus, but the policemen eventually overwhelmed the men. Angus MacDonald was arrested and taken to the police station, where he was bound hand and foot. While he lay helpless on the floor, MacLennan proceeded to kick him repeatedly in the body, causing considerable injury. MacLennan was later charged with this but got off with a fine. (16)

"The Fiscal was sent for, the Sheriff-Clerk, and the Sheriff himself, the Riot Act was read; and altogether they lodged the terrible man from Bernera in jail!" reported *The Highlander*. The large crowd was dispersed, and when everything settled down Angus MacDonald's companions hurried back to Bernera to report his predicament. When the men reached Garynahine they were asked by the local policeman what the trouble was; they told him he would likely hear all about it in the morning. (17)

In Bernera the news sparked off a spontaneous show of resistance among a beleaguered people. And anyone who showed reluctance to act was rounded on by Donald MacDonald (Domhnall MacNèill, nicknamed Dan) who called the people to riot. He told a Bosta man: "Bi 'n-àird, tha thusa glè bhlàth agus cofhurtail ann an sin 's do nàbaidh air leacan fuara ann am prìosan Steòrnabhaigh." (18) Boats were dispatched to Carloway and to Uig to raise more men. In Valtos Donald MacRitchie (An Irish) left his work at the corn mill and rounded up every available man. (19) Piper Donald MacLennan from Cnip led the Uig contingent, they met the Bernera men at Garynahine. (20) A total of 150 men gathered, they were given meat, bread and a dram before heading towards town.

Later, during the march it was Donald MacDonald (Dan) who made sure their unity of purpose remained intact. The plan was to use a yacht mast of pitched pine to ram the prison doors. *The Highlander* reported:"The sound of the bagpipes heralded from a distance the approach of a band of Bernera men, perhaps 150 strong, marching steadily, four abreast, to enforce their own claims." (21)

When the Stornoway legal establishment realised what was happening they supplied MacDonald with a new suit of clothing and hastily released him. They expected his release to calm the marchers and dissuade them from entering the town. Again it was Dan who insisted they continue as planned. They mustered at Manor

Lady Matheson is reputed to have served tea and biscuits to the Bernera rioters in the conservatory of the Lews Castle.

Park where the Sheriff-Clerk, the Fiscal and Police Superintendent Donald Cameron urged them to go home — but to no avail. The marchers spent the night at Goathill and proceeded to the castle in the morning. They elected Angus MacArthur as their speaker.

When the marchers confronted Sir James Matheson at the castle he denied any knowledge of the events in Bernera. He claimed that the factor Munro had kept him in the dark, but promised to look into the matter so long as they went home in peace. He said he would sent valuators to the island to provide a report on the case. Lady Matheson then gave the marchers tea in the conservatory. (22)

A few weeks later Angus MacDonald, Norman MacAulay and John MacLeod were summoned to appear in court, and trial was set for July 17th. Quite contrary to the assurances given on the lawns of Lews Castle, there was no communication between Sir James Matheson and his Bernera tenants before or after the trial.

But it was the trial, and in particular the superb advocacy of Charles Innes, which exposed the remarkable powers Matheson had vested in his factor, and Munro's tyranny in dealing with the Lewis crofters. Innes's summing-up at the end of the trial was a masterpiece, which encapsulated not only the specific circumstances which gave rise to the charges but also the wider picture of life in Lewis under Matheson and Munro. By the time of the trial, Munro had been removed by the Sheriff from his position as Fiscal and it may be that his successor in that role, William Ross, was by no means displeased to see the factor in the witness-box and morally in the dock. (23) Certainly, Mr Ross raised no objection to Innes's wide-ranging approach to the case. "I have thought it right," Innes told the jury, "to go into these matters in order that you might clearly understand the cause and origin of the disagreement which culminated in the occurrence which has necessitated our presence here today."

He went over the forced move to Earshader, the building of the dyke and then the notice to move once again without offer of compensation. "The new lands were less in extent than the old, necessitating a reduction of stock, notwithstanding which it was hinted, a rise of rent was to take place. In point of fact, the promised land was not a land of promise. Negotiations were once again entered upon, and the poor crofters were cajoled and threatened in turn, and, for a change, coaxed and bullied." (24)

The effects of the summonses if implemented would have been "the turning out of house and home of several hundreds of human beings." Innes invited the jury to judge whether or not Munro was to be believed when "he says that his including the houses and crofts was a mere matter of form." He continued: "From the way in which these poor people have been treated, one would be naturally led to suppose that they were undesirable tenants. But though repeatedly asked by me, the chamberlain who was also for many years the Procurator Fiscal — an office from which the Sheriff has now very properly removed him — could not give one single instance in which any one from Bernera was accused during the last twenty years of

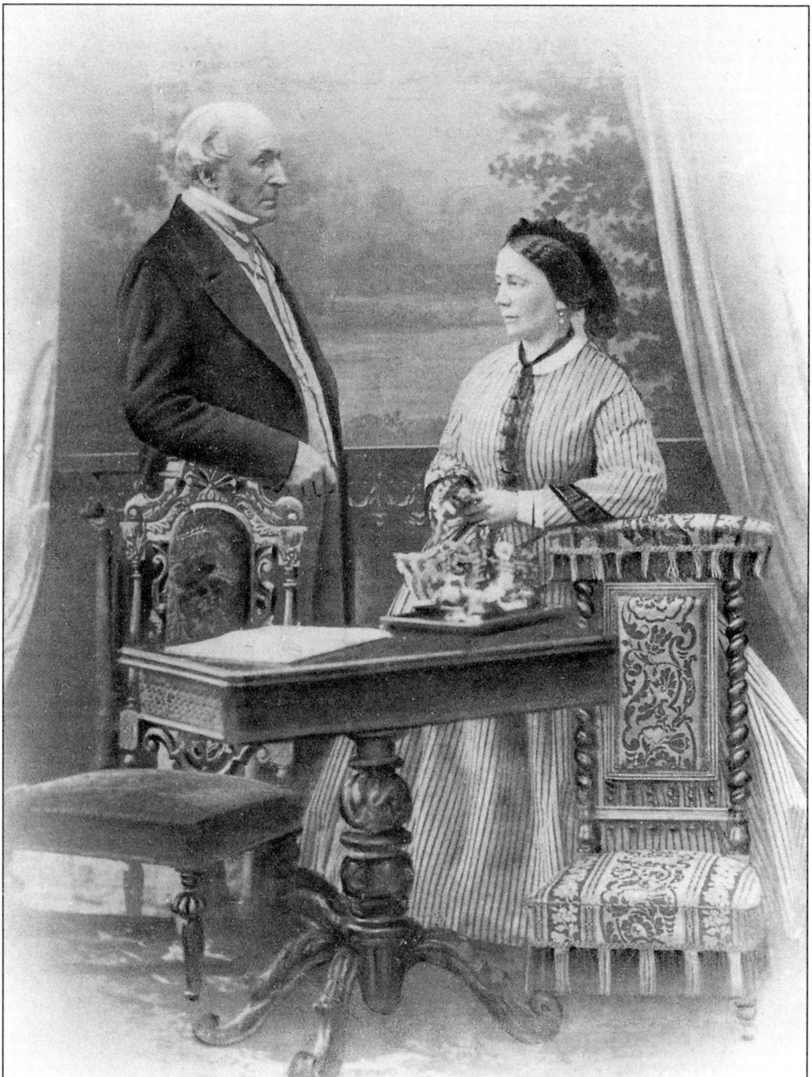

© Collection of Duncan Morison

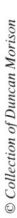

Sir James and Lady Matheson.

having committed any crime."

Innes, having painted a glowing picture of the Bernera people, then turned to the regime under which they lived: "Such a system of management as seems to prevail here is calculated to call forth cries as to tenant-right and fixity of tenure, which if once raised will spread over to the mainland and as was found in Ireland, will not easily be allayed. It used to be said that the slave who breathed the air of Britain immediately became free; but from what one hears, and from what has come out in evidence in this case, I fear very much that that could not be said of this island at the present moment, for it appears to me that there are many poor but deserving men here who can hardly call their souls their own..." (25)

Innes had turned the entire case around. No longer were the men in the dock on trial, but the system which persecuted them and their fellows. He then started to take the character of Munro to pieces, using the deadliest of weapons — ridicule. "In this court, looking to the nature of his multifarious offices, I can almost fancy it is possible for him to appear at one and the same time in the capacity of prosecutor, judge and jury. It is, in point of fact, a matter of great difficulty, if not impossibility to think in the singular of such a great pluralist."

Warming to his theme, Innes declared: "Had this island never been united to the neighbouring islands of Great Britain and Ireland, and had Mr Munro been king *de jure*, he really would not be the great man he is, occupying, as he does, the position merely *de facto*. Then he would have Houses of Parliament and Cabinet Ministers to control him, but now there is no man to say nay; his power seems to be absolute; his word seems to be law; the people seem to quake and tremble at his approach, his very nod conveys a meaning neither you nor I could convey in a sentence."

Having characterised Munro as "the oppressor" of Bernera, and reflected on the factor's good fortune not to be operating in Ireland, Innes declared: "I trust the effect of this trial will be that oppression will cease. Whether it does or not, I have no doubt that the people of these islands will continue to be what they are and always have been — a law-abiding people." Having declared this massive indictment of the system, Innes turned his attention to the particulars of the case. But it was these general remarks which surely finished Munro and ensured that the Bernera case would become such a landmark in crofting history. (26)

Innes went on to ridicule the scale of the incident which had occurred as the Sheriff Officer and his little party had left Tobson. "He talked today of the crowd by which they were pursued and the consequent terror felt by him; but the exciseman told us that the crowd consisted of five or six people, some of whom were children... The whole occurrence, no doubt, arose from a desire on the part of some of the high-spirited youth of Tobson to resent MacRae's offensive manner. None of the officer's party was injured, but MacLennan seems to have felt that his dignity was offended... He seems to be a hot-headed, impudent person; and he told his companions if he had his rifle he would have made some of the women of Bernera resent the loss of their sons."

By the next day, Innes recounted, MacLennan was still uttering the same threat in the hearing of the three people he still had eviction notices to serve upon. The young men of Bernera, preparing to go out to the fishing, decided to confront him over the threats. They included the three accused. MacLennan had been "forced to admit in cross-examination that they had not laid a hand upon any part of his person, and that he was in no way injured. He was alarmed, of course just as cowards always are, but he did not say anything on that occasion about using his rifle — he was wise for once." Innes told the jury: "You have now before you a true and full account of what has come to be known as the Great Bernera Riot." He appealed to them only to rely upon their "own good conscience" without reference to what "may be pleasing to the Powers-that-be and rule in this island."

After Sheriff Spittal had summed up, the packed courtroom awaited the verdict of the jury who were unable to gain access to the jury-room because of the crowded scenes. They conferred briefly in the box before the foreman, a Mr MacPherson, rose to say: "My Lord, the jury unanimously find the panels not guilty." (27)

Munro's rule over Lewis was broken. Sir James Matheson's stewardship of the island had been laid bare for history to judge. A turning-point had been reached in the history of the Highlands and Islands.

On Bernera the immediate effect of the Riot and its aftermath was the dropping of the evictions, while the people continued to use the old grazings. Over the years which followed, some concessions were made to the Bernera people by the estate. For example, they acceded to a request for more land by the villagers of Bosta. Five years after the Riot, the Bosta people were given Kirkibost and in the winter of 1879 they carried the roofs of the old dwellings to their new village, built new houses and later took in the land. Without the Riot, these people would have been off on emigrant ships.

However the sense of injustice, based on land hunger when so much of their surroundings lay empty and idle, survived. The last attempt on Bernera to take more land into crofting was in 1901, when six Tobson crofters took possession of Croir, which had been leased to Malcolm MacDonald in 1880, but had previously been in crofting tenure. The raiders wrote to the Congested Districts Board: "There are 43 souls of us. Surely our lives are of more account than that of one man, or of 100 sheep." (28) It was a long struggle before they finally obtained legal access to the land.

All these events remain alive in the island folk memory, and shaped the communities which exist today. Bernera suffered clearances under the Seaforths and again under Matheson. In 1851, those who remained had seen 400 beleaguered souls bundled onto the emigrant ships in the Sound of Bernera. For the island of Bernera, the stand taken in the form of the Bernera Riot, was the turning-point and the guarantor of a continuing crofting population. But its significance went much wider, and represented a crucial first step in the movement towards security of tenure for the whole crofting community.

Notes and References

1. This is strongly the belief of local folk history. The Bernera Riot is also referred to in the early song of Màiri Mhòr nan Oran, the great poetess of the land law reform movement.

2. J. Hunter, *The Making of the Crofting Community*, Edinburgh, 1976.

3. *The Oban Times,* June, 1874.

4. J. Shaw Grant, *A Shilling for Your Scowl,* Stornoway, 1992.

5. D. MacKinlay, *The Island of Lewis and its Fishermen-Crofters,* London, 1878.

6. Charles Innes was born in Inverness and was trained as a lawyer at the University of Edinburgh. In 1863 he was assumed into partnership by Charles Fraser-MacIntosh, who was to become a leading figure in the Highland land reform movement, and was one of the five radical pro-crofter MPs elected in 1885.

7. The cattle were summered on the moors, the women and young girls left the villages for six weeks, driving the cattle out to the shielings and sending milk, butter and cheese into the villages each week.

8. *The Bernera Riot,* Edinburgh, 1874. The booklet contains verbatim transcripts of the trial and was republished by Dòmhnall MacCormaig, Edinburgh, 1981.

9. Ibid.

10. The villages between Scaliscro and Bernera were cleared during the Seaforth era.

11. D. MacKinlay, *The Island of Lewis and its Fishermen-Crofters,* London, 1878.

12. The summonses were received in shocked silence. The Reverend Donald MacAulay, Kirkibost, told me that the image passed down through the generations was one of overwhelming sadness which later turned to bitterness and anger.

13. *The Oban Times,* September, 1874.

14. Although nobody was seriously injured, it was believed to have been considerably more violent than reported.

15. It is believed locally that the two men who escaped spent the night at the town's curing houses, and that the fish-curers encouraged the men to riot — they strongly supported some form of action against Munro.

16. I am indebted to Joan MacIver and Calum MacDonald, Kinlochroag, and the Reverend Donald MacAulay, Kirkibost, for providing detailed local knowledge of the event.

17. On their return from Stornoway, the men hinted at the planned action before they reached Bernera, which suggested that the Riot was not spontaneous.

18. "Get up. You are warm and comfortable in your bed while your neighbour lies on the cold slabs of Stornoway prison."

19. When he was in his sixties, Malcolm MacRitchie, "An Irish," from Valtos, was one of the men arrested for raiding the farm of Reef.

20. The piper Donald MacLennan, Kneep, was presented with a watch by the Bernera villagers for leading the contingent to Stornoway.

21. *The Highlander,* April, 1874.

22. D. MacKinlay, *The Island of Lewis and its Fishermen-Crofters,* London, 1878.

23. William Ross, the Procurator Fiscal had family connections in Bernera. This is thought to have been a factor in the treatment of the men on trial.

24. *The Bernera Riot,* Edinburgh, 1874.

25. Ibid.

26. Although Charles Innes was himself a Tory, he was partner in the firm of Charles Fraser-MacIntosh who later became one of the Crofter MPs for Inverness-shire.

27. *The Bernera Riot, Edinburgh, 1874.*

28. *Highland News,* April, 1901.

2 The Park Deer Raid

"On the face of the deserted villages, once the happy homes of the free and the brave, now lying in silent desolation, we read: 'The scourge of Landlordism has passed over us.'"

> Rev. Donald MacCallum in his evidence to
> the Deer Forest Commission, 1892.

"My father was the only one of my grandfather's family who did not emigrate... My nephew, who came across here a few years ago, used to tell me this; that when people gathered from all parts, the Highland people, the burden of their conversation was the old homes they had left behind, and they all used to say that if they could, they would return back again."

> John Smith, Keose, giving evidence to the Napier Commission, 1883.

"It is reported here that the crofters of various townships are not a little put out about the new shooting lodge which is now being created at Eishken Park. The crofters have unanimously resolved to give ample warning to Mr Platt, that he need never expect to be permitted to be the shooting tenant of the Park Forest for the following reasons: that 600 inhabitants are nearly starving for want of larger holdings while the whole 600 are kept in poverty so as to gratify the sporting propensities of one single individual."

> *The Oban Times,* February, 18th, 1866.

In September 1887, the Highland Land League held its annual meeting in Oban. One of the delegates, Donald MacRae of Balallan, aroused the antennae of the press by boldly declaring: "In my district winged game have disappeared, and the deer will follow, as the crofters are to have venison along with their potatoes this winter." (1)

Since his arrival at Balallan as headmaster, Donald MacRae had been organising crofter meetings in the school. They brought people from the whole parish of Lochs together, to discuss landlessness and the appalling economic conditions which prevailed. Already known as the "Alness Martyr" MacRae had been relieved of his

Crofters' houses near Balallan, Lochs District.

Entrance to Loch Shell.

position as Rosskeen School in Easter Ross because of his sympathy for the crofters' cause. (2) His arrival at Balallan where he immediately identified with the plight of the crofting community was seen as a "kindly act of providence" by the people of Lochs.

After MacRae's Oban declaration, warning shots were immediately fired from the Scottish Office. "The Oban meeting was contemptible," wrote the Secretary of State, Lord Lothian, and asked to be supplied with all the particulars of the Balallan delegate. Lothian did, however, concede that things were very bad in Lewis, and feared that the only solution — assistance to emigrate — would be a costly one for the Government. Emigration, he insisted, was the course of action which "so many of the Lewis people want." (3)

While the incumbents of Dover House set about hatching yet another emigration scheme for the troublesome Highlanders, an event which has gone down in history as a magnificent act of resistance was being organised by the people of Lochs who could otherwise see no future for themselves or their children, but debilitating poverty and want. If matters were to improve, they desperately needed the land from which their forebears had been systematically removed forty and fifty years earlier. This time they would not be bundled onto the emigrant ship.

Within the parish of Lochs, in the South-East of the Isle of Lewis, the peninsula of Park, or South Lochs extends to 68,000 acres. Until the beginning of the 19th century the whole of it was inhabited, with the population distributed through more than thirty small townships. South Park was systematically cleared between 1818 and 1843 while the grazier Donald Stewart and his brothers held the lease and the whole of Lewis was still under the ownership of the Seaforths. (4)

Valamus, Ceann Chrionaig, Ceannmore and the other small townships in Southern Park were the first cleared, to make a sheep farm established by Lord Seaforth around Valamus. The sheep farm continued to grow until eventually it covered two-thirds of the entire peninsula stretching from Loch Erisort in the north to Loch Seaforth in the South. An estimated 400 people were cleared during that period and by 1843 the area south of Gravir was left devoid of people. Later, in 1858, the deserted village of Lemreway was resettled. But by 1886 up to 50,000 acres of the peninsula had been removed from crofting, with the remaining population crowded onto the small portion left to the crofters. Many more were driven off to Canada and still others re-settled in townships all over the island.

When Sir James Matheson bought the island in 1844 the clearance of Park was well under way. By 1851, after the hardships of the famine years the people lived and did relatively well by the fishing. They were able to pay their rents, and that was the foremost consideration on the part of the Matheson estate. John Munro MacKenzie, the Matheson chamberlain, was unusually gleeful when he finished collecting the rents for the parish in September 1851. "Left Lochs," he wrote, "much

View near Balallan, Lochs District.

pleased with the people seeing that they had done their best to pay the rents and upward of 100 closed their accounts."

Habost, Garyvard, Torastaigh, Caverstaigh, Cromore, Gravir, Marvig, Kershader and Calbost — the handful of communities which remained in Park — were fishing villages. Munro MacKenzie wrote: "They make well of the herring fishing at Stornoway and Wick, having good boats and nets. Almost every tenant is a part-owner of a boat. It is a pleasure to see the readiness and goodwill with which these people pay their rents." It is remarkable, and a measure of the man, that this is the only entry in the year-long diary in which he expresses any form of satisfaction. During his time as factor, the parish was lotted and people were given 15 year leases over their croft holdings. But as usual the allocation of leases and their retention were subject to certain conditions. Rents were increased; there was an obligation on the part of the tenants to improve crofts and houses; children were to be kept at school; and 'statute labour' was to be paid to the landlord.

In the latter half of the 19th century the population grew at a natural pace. It was sustained, mainly, by the fishing. At the same time, however, grazings were once again being removed and the land available to the increasing population became less and less. The crofters sub-divided their holdings to make room for the young married couples; this process led to the crofts being shared among three or four households.

The story of Balallan — a village in Lochs bordering on the Park area — as expressed to the Napier Commission in 1883 illustrates the process, common to crofting townships all over the Highlands, during this period. Under the Seaforths, when John Knox was factor, Kintarvay which was part of the Balallan hill pasture, was taken and added to the sporting ground of Aline. Then, when the Park crofters were dispossessed of their lands, 16 families, 60 or more people, were placed in Balallan. Airidh Bhruaich was also part of the Balallan grazings before it was taken and a village formed there. When John Munro MacKenzie became factor, he divided Balallan into 64 crofts, where there were previously only 26 lots, and increased the rent. His successor as factor Donald Munro also increased the rents. By 1886, 32 families were without land in the village; the rest were grossly over-crowded, and the land available to the village for grazing had been steadily reduced. The only possible result was poverty, which had been systematically created out of relative plenty. (6)

In all of the Park district by 1881, 1,700 people were crowded into nine villages with 181 crofts. In most villages cottars and crofters alike tried to survive on an average of half an acre each of inbye land both arable and pasture. The land under crofting was being steadily eroded, while the landlord continued to seek new ways of squeezing more money out of the tenantry. The system of taxation additional to the basic rent, even by the 1880s, bore the stamp of feudalism. Additional assessments included rent for moorland pasture, usually four or five shillings, then there was the poor rate, the doctor's rate, the school rate and hen money — which was the feudal kain obligation, converted into cash — and road money, even although there were very few roads.

Kenneth MacDonald, Leurbost, outlined these additional burdens to the Napier Commission. "When the Road Act was passed five shillings were added to the rent and hen money. Double renting commenced in 1870; fine for Cleascro plantation fence in 1871; fine for Arnish deer forest fence in 1873; double poor rate paid in 1868. Two girls and three boys were taken to the Fiscal's office for taking oysters out of the ebb; mussels and winkles were taxed. Those taxes were collected by Donald MacDonald, crofter constable, Balallan." In other words, every device at the landlord's disposal was used to screw a few more shillings out of a subsistence tenantry.

To some extent the growing certainty of wholesale impoverishment, through the creation of these conditions, was disguised during the 1860s and 1870s, when agricultural prices were good. Expansion of the east coast and domestic fisheries provided the essential supplementary cash revenue for the crofters, but it was a precarious balance and when it tipped against them, the full impact of the changes which had been evolving and the new burdens which had been imposed upon them, meant that the people found themselves facing perennial debt as well as worsening living conditions.

By the early 1880s, the price of cattle had dropped and there was a glut of herring on the market. In addition the fish curers changed their operations so that the fishermen had to sell their catch on the open market. This did away with the traditional wage structure, with each hired hand only getting a portion of the daily cash proceeds. (7) In Lewis an estimated £40,000 was lost from poor fishing returns during 1887. Things were no better on the east coast, where Lewis fishermen traditionally spent part of the year. A glut of herring depressed prices and instead of bringing back £10-£30 from the east coast season, fishermen were returning with as little as £1-£3. The poor fishing returns caused meal dealers and merchants to suspend credit. Crisis was clearly on the horizon.

In December 1887, John Cheyne in a report to the Secretary of State for Scotland, commented: "In the parish of Lochs there is a most lamentable state of destitution, if not amongst the crofters, at least amongst the cottars and squatters who depend almost entirely on what they earn at the fishing which was this season extremely unremunerative..." (8) It was apparent that the only solution for the population was access to an adequate portion of land, which would cushion the blow when the fishing failed. More land was needed anyway, to ease the strain both on the people and on the over-worked arable and pasture.

The people of Lochs were fully aware of an impending crisis and tried as early as November 1881 to avert it. The lease of the Park sheep farm was up for renewal in 1883 and the local population of Marvig, Calbost and Gravir petitioned the widowed

Shooting Lodge at Eishken, Loch Shell.

proprietrix, Lady Matheson, for a portion of the land. Anxious to get their claim in first, they wrote: "At present we are either squatters or hold small patches of land from other crofters in these villages, all of which are inadequate for the support of ourselves and our families. Unless some means are devised to extend our holdings ... we must either have to emigrate or become a burden upon the estate." (9) The former townships of Orinsaigh and Stiomrabhaigh, low-lying and adjacent to the sea would satisfy their demands. And they assured the estate that the land they wanted would not "militate against or depreciate the farm for shooting, sporting and other purposes."

The petitioners also challenged the estate's assertion, that the land of Park was unsuitable for cultivation. "We remember the men that left it. They were old men when we were boys, and to the day of their death they used to mourn their removal from Park, and wished to go back to it; so that if the quite sufficient land there is fairly and wisely distributed there is plenty of room to make a living in our own land." (10) And to this plea for redress, the ungracious Lady Matheson did not take the trouble to respond.

A year passed and the petitioners tried again. The second petition was accompanied by a letter which ended with the words "...trusting we may not be led to resort reluctantly to such steps as many of our unfortunate countrymen are forced to adopt."

In January 1883 they got their response from the Matheson residence in Cleveland Row, London. "Lady Matheson regrets that the above named respectable Lewismen should have been led to address her on a subject of such importance as that contained in their petition, by adding it to a letter, which causes her to set aside their request, as Lady Matheson is too devoted to her Queen and the laws of which Her Gracious Majesty is the representative, to listen for one moment to a petition accompanied by a threat from them to infringe the laws by which we are all governed." (11)

A few months later the sheep farm of Park was advertised and let as one unit, without any small tenants. The agricultural lease had been held by the son of the notorious Patrick Sellar, who ruthlessly executed the Sutherland Clearances. Ironically it was in 1886, the year of the Crofters Act which for the first time gave crofters security of tenure and a fair rent, that the 42,000 acre expanse of Park was let as a deer forest — to Joseph Platt, an English machine maker and his wife Jessie, who was a member of the aristocratic Thorneycroft family. A Mr. W.H. Brackner held the neighbouring Aline deer forest lease.

The Crofters Act of 1886 was, and still is, the most fundamental piece of legislation in crofting history. It laid out the basis of crofting rights and provided security of tenure in perpetuity. But in spite of the relentless efforts of the Crofter MPs, the Act had major shortcomings. In particular, it utterly failed to address the growing problem of landlessness in the Highlands. In the parish of Lochs by the late 1880s there were up to 300 families without land and squatting on other people's already overburdened crofts.

The years of relative economic stability were at an end. The Fraser Report of 1888 commented that for two successive seasons "hundreds, nay thousands have returned from the East Coast, several penniless." The story of Murdo MacDonald of Balallan was pitifully typical. He had brought back only £1 from the east coast. Almost all of that had gone on meal, and on paying off debt. There was no work, they had nothing to eat but potatoes from their neighbours, there were six children in the family. (12) Living in these awful conditions cheek by jowl with a huge tract of land devoted to the sporting whims of the gentry was, to say the very least, grossly offensive.

It was the poverty, the short-comings of the Crofters Act, and the gross misuse of land around them which combined to convince the crofters of Lochs that they must act. The grounds for discontent had been accumulating over decades. But now the hopelessness of their circumstances seemed particularly acute, with no relief in sight. Leadership had arrived in the person of Donald MacRae. The scene was set for the march on the forest of Park in November 1887.

General view of Loch Shell from Eishken Lodge.

The Raid

"My age is 63 years; I came to Laxay at the age of eight, along with my father and another ten crofters, who were driven away with all their belongings from their thriving and agreeable holdings at Aline and Park, in which they knew nothing beyond prosperity and happiness.

"Park, which nature seems to mean for man, with its arable lands, hill pasture, and bays of the sea ... was relieved of its inhabitant population... To the perpetrators of such deeds the discontentment and bitter feelings of the fugitive inhabitants appeared as nothing at all compared with the peculiar pleasure they enjoyed from the fact that now the sheep and the fleet-footed deer could graze on the meadows and on the heaths so impiously depopulated."

George MacKenzie, Laxay, Evidence to the Napier Commission, 1883.

"It is the cottars' turn now... They not only demand the restoration of Park, but all the other lands under the sheep and deer, with compensation for the loss suffered by themselves and their fathers through the conduct of the evictors who ruled them and left them landless in pauperism."

The Oban Times, December, 1887.

"The raid... is not one invited by oppression. It is due to no hard treatment on the part of the owner or the tenant of the forest. It is the outcome of bad advice — the result of that praise of disorder which has become the gospel of Gladstone Liberals since they became the close allies and apologists of Parnellism."

The Scotsman, November 24th, 1887.

On the 11th November 1887, people from all corners of North and South Lochs gathered in Balallan and resolved that "groups of crofters and cottars, principally the latter, should leave the various townships and meet at a place half-way between Balallan and Eishken, then to proceed into the forests of Park, in one body, and shoot all the deer they might come across or drive them into the sea." (13)

After making these arrangements for the 22nd of the month the crofters invited the Sheriff, the lessee of Park and the proprietrix to visit their homes to see for themselves the conditions in which they lived. Sheriff Fraser at first agreed to go, but on November 18th he wrote declining the invitation, fearing that the object of his visit to Lochs might be misconstrued. Subsequently, however, he saw Donald MacRae who outlined details of the planned raid and told the Sheriff that unless the starving people were supplied with meal the raid would go ahead. The Sheriff, who appears to have been a sympathetic man, said he had no authority to provide meal. The raid would thus go ahead, with the full knowledge of the authorities.

On the evening of the 20th November, the steam yacht *Transit* which belonged to Joseph Platt arrived at Stornoway from Eishken. On board were Sheriff Fraser and John Ross, the Procurator Fiscal. *The Scotsman* reported that nothing had transpired as a result of the Sheriff's visit to Lochs, and that no police constables were to be sent to the area. It seems that very few were ready to believe that the threats so freely made would be carried out.

Only two days later, on 22nd November, 1887, confirmation was provided that the Balallan resolutions were indeed serious. The men of Lochs marched with pipers at their head and with their flags raised high, into the Park forest. In a panicky telegram to Dover House the Stornoway Sheriff Substitute, Alexander Fraser, reported: "Two hundred men with rifles, tents, banners and provisions have entered the Deer Forest and threatened to remain until all the deer are exterminated. They will listen to no remonstrance." (14)

The Dingwall-based Chief Constable, John Cheyne, lost no time in demanding the assistance of a gunboat and marines. Within hours of the news of the raid he had requisitioned a detachment of Royal Scots based at the Maryhill Barracks in Glasgow. Cheyne wrote to the Secretary of State for Scotland: "I hope to cross with them to Stornoway, and I hope that their mere presence will bring the poor misguided people to their senses." (15) The sense of drama which was rapidly developing among the authorities was greatly added to by the shrill demands of Mrs Jessie Platt, wife of the Park deer forest lessee, "Delay may be fatal," she telegraphed the Scottish Office portentously.

In order to attract as much publicity as possible, the raiders informed the press of their intentions, prior to going into the forest. Eye-witness accounts therefore appeared in all the national newspapers. The first reports appeared in the *North British Daily Mail,* a Glasgow-based Liberal and staunchly pro-crofter paper, and in *The Oban Times* which in that era had been a great friend to the Highland crofters throughout their struggles. *The Scotsman* and *The Glasgow Herald* were in the opposite camp, equally staunchly pro-Establishment, but in all of these papers, no matter what angle the leaders took, the verbatim accounts of the reporters are invaluable. There is little disagreement about the facts of what transpired.

Early on the morning of the assigned day, horns sounded in each village to signal the start of the raid. The first two groups of 40 men left Balallan at daybreak and met with a contingent of 120 who marched from the direction of Glen Gravir. A piper led each contingent; they carried with them sails for tents, provisions, rifles

Loch Seaforth Head, showing the hills driven for deer.

and a number of flags. As they passed through the villages the old men, women and children cheered them on their way.

Just before the raiders entered the forest they were stopped by Mrs Jessie Platt and her head gamekeeper Murdo MacRae. Mrs Platt urged the men to stop but they passed her by with the immortal words: "We have no English my Lady." Murdo MacRae pleaded with the men: "An ann às ur ciall a tha sibh?" When there was no response from the marchers, Mr Macrae continued: "Cò tha air ur ceann?" Seonaidh 'an Oig, Cromore replied: "Tha ar bonaidean," and continued into the forest. Meanwhile the fishing boats, the *Daisy* and *Star* left Marvig and headed for inner Loch Seaforth with meal and peats for the raiders. They were afterwards used to carry the deer carcasses to the villages. (16)

Each one of the raiders had been assigned a particular duty. Some were to drive the deer into the range of the guns while the best shots killed the deer. They were accompanied by men whose job it was to carry the carcasses, and the remainder bore the provisions to camp. When it became apparent that the raid was in progress, 15 of the Platt employees attempted to scatter the deer and keep them out of the firing range.

The first night the entire force encamped opposite Airidh Bhruaich. *The Scotsman* reporter prevailed upon Donald MacRae, the Balallan schoolmaster, to accompany him to the camp, ostensibly to act as interpreter. It was a cold and still November night and the bright moonlight helped the men negotiate the way. They borrowed a small boat at Airidh Bhruaich, and as they approached the shore near the camp site, other small boats could be seen ferrying men and carcasses across the loch.

The Scotsman reported: "The scene was the most impressive, and not a sound broke the stillness save the swish of the oars. Suddenly sweeping round a point the gleaming of firelight was seen, and the camp thus showed its position. 'What boat is that?' was asked in Gaelic, and on the response of 'friends' being made we piled onto the beach about 100 yards from the camp."

The large tent, made of cabers covered with canvas boat sails, was pitched within a few yards of Airidh Dhòmhnaill Chaim, nestling against the magnificent backdrop of the Silver Hill (Sìthean an Airgid) and Mòr Monadh. Five watchfires burned in front of the tent, while inside the pipers played and a bountiful supper was prepared. In *The Old and the New Highlands & Hebrides* James Cameron paints a vivid picture of the scene:

"The night was one of the loveliest and in every way favourable to the raiders. The scene was of such an extraordinary character that there is no other in Highland history, at any rate since Culloden, to compare with it.

"A camp, 100 yards long illuminated with five peat fires, each as large as a haystack. Over the one in the centre was suspended a magnificent specimen of a Royal Stag. Within yards of this fire there was another of equal size above which

Park raiders leaving the deer forest.

there was the carcass of a deer broiling, and there was an immense cauldron with Irish stew.

"Behind these fires there were raiders sitting in couches of heather and stone, pretty much in the fashion of their forefathers when they roamed the ancient forests of old Caledonia. Some were eating, others attending the fires, others chanting songs mostly from Duncan Ban McIntyre — Chunna mi 'n damh donn 's na h-èildean — and others.

"On the approach of strangers no attempt was made to stop them; on the contrary they were asked to listen to the cause which induced them to resort to such methods of hunting for food, and to invite them to partake of a share of what was going.

"Then there was the dramatic effect of the white-headed patriarch from Marvig. Alastair Tharmoid, Alastair MacFarlane, standing bare headed with his back to the blazing peat fire, with uplifted swarthy hands invoking a blessing, in rich sonorous Gaelic upon the venison festival. The subject was worthy of the brush of the immortal Rembrandt, the master of light and shade."

On the second day of the raid Sheriff Fraser and James Gordon, Chief Superintendent of Police, caught up with some of the raiders at Ruadh Chleit. There were about 40 men with eight guns among them. The Sheriff spoke to the raiders in Gaelic asking them to give up the hunt and go home. They refused, and once again told of their grievances and the necessity of their action; other means of redress had been sought, and turned down. This was the last resort and they were driven by desperation. The Riot Act was read to the men and its terms explained in Gaelic. The raiders, worn out, turned and headed for home, signalling the end of the raid.

In the early evening boats were seen heading towards Gravir and Marvig in South Park. Most of the men withdrew from the forest before nightfall. The raid had ended peacefully. The people of Lochs had, in a superbly effective manner, put their case to the nation — a fact reflected in the massive media coverage and subsequent Parliamentary attention given to the raid. They had been pushed to the abyss of poverty and injustice and had fought back in the only way open to them.

The Military and the Arrests

"The military again for the Highlands. The old Tory dodge. The unfortunate people starve, and the Tory Government to their cry for meal answer bullets."

Letter from R.P. Cunningham-Graham MP,
North British Daily Mail, November 24th, 1887.

"The greatest naval demonstration that had taken place on the part of this country since bombardment of Alexandria — they had five ships of war threatening the Isle of Lewis."

Dr. Cameron MP, addressing the House of Commons,
February 21st, 1888.

On receiving news of the Park raid, the War Office sanctioned the use of *HMS Ajax*, and it left Greenock for Stornoway with 100 marines on board on 24th November. She, however, broke down en route. *HMS Seahorse* left Portsmouth the following day, and the Fishery Board was ordered to make *HMS Jackal* available for duty in the Hebrides. Three other naval ships — the *Belleisle*, *Amelia* and *Forester* — joined the armada. For good measure, the Royal Mail steamer, *Locheil*, was commandeered to take the Royal Scots from Strome Ferry to Stornoway. (17)

When news of the end of the raid reached the Lord Advocate he immediately wrote to Lord Lothian recommending that the military preparations continue. "It would be unwise to make any changes until sufficient arrests have been made to vindicate the law. Our intention as regards the arrests — to have those arrested indicted at once and get them tried before Xmas, as promptitude is of much importance in this case as is severe sentences. Of course, the question of punishment is for the Court, but I hope for the sake of the Highland people themselves, that the judges will recognise that the lesson of the last years — convictions with mild sentences — has not provided the results hoped for." (18)

Stornoway was alive with policemen. But the authorities were being canny. Determined to avoid a repetition of the 'fiasco' of crofters defying the police as they had done on Skye the previous year during Sheriff Ivory's infamous expedition, the police on this occasion were to take no action until the Marines arrived as back-up. The raiders were to be given a chance to surrender voluntarily, and those who did not come forward would be rounded up by the combined forces of the military and the police.

The military detachments arrived off the mail steamer the Locheil, at midnight on Friday.

Soldiers crossing to Stornoway, keeping themselves warm.

Cheyne, the Ross-shire Chief Constable, joined the high powered military team of Captain Farquharson, Lieutenants Pritchard, Munro and MacFarlane and Surgeon Leishman of the Army Hospital Corps, at Dingwall, and proceeded with them to Stornoway.

In spite of the large police and military presence only two constables were sent to Lochs, and in fact that proved sufficient. The raiders had made it clear from the outset that if any law was violated they would willingly surrender. Police Sergeant Hector Smith, himself a native of Keose in Lochs, offered to return to Stornoway with the men — without the aid of military or the police. Sergeant Smith was a shrewd man, and went with schoolmaster Donald MacRae to the homes of the wanted men from Balallan; he then gave the policeman a note for the men of South Lochs asking them to follow the example of their neighbours and to give themselves up.

Sixteen men were charged, including Donald MacRae. Even although he had not participated in the raid, the authorities were determined to convict him of inciting agitation. The charge was based on a Gaelic speech MacRae had delivered in the schoolhouse at a meeting of the Land League, which was apparently attended by Eishken estate workers. Ross, the Procurator Fiscal, went especially to Balallan to pick up MacRae and Roderick MacKenzie a merchant from the village, who was a member of the Balallan school board and a prominent Land League activist. Both men were imprisoned and bail set at £60. They were later released, bail in respect of Donald MacRae being paid by Mr Malcolm MacLeod, president of the Stornoway Land League and Mr Alex MacAulay. Mr Roderick MacKenzie of the Crown Inn, Stornoway, put up bail for the merchant. (19)

All of the others 'arrested' in such an informal manner made their way to the police station where they were charged with mobbing, rioting and intimidation. They declined to answer any questions put to them, except to provide their names and addresses. The men were then imprisoned and bail set at £40.

Donald MacFarlane, who had been the pro-crofter MP for Argyllshire in the first Gladstone administration in 1886, offered to put up bail for the imprisoned raiders. A General Election campaign was in progress at the time of the Park raid, and Malcolm MacLeod, president of the Lewis Land League team, telegraphed MacFarlane saying that he feared his offer would have an effect on his candidacy in Argyll. In response, MacFarlane wrote: "I have no fear of compromising myself. I have no opinion about the case but do not want the men imprisoned before the trial. Offer bail in my name." (20)

In Edinburgh the Lord Advocate continued to influence the course of justice. In a telegram to Lord Lothian he suggested that only the "instigators be sent for trial; they are the worst criminals and as the raiders are poor and ignorant it might be best to promptly have them tried summarily and disposed of, leaving jury trial for those who have led them into this." (21)

The gun-boat, Jackal, Loch Leurbost.

Accordingly, of the 16 men arrested only six were sent for trial to the High Court in Edinburgh. They were Donald MacRae, Balallan; Roderick MacKenzie, merchant, 46 Balallan; John Matheson, 13 Gravir; Murdo MacDonald, 61 Balallan; Malcolm MacKenzie, 26 Crossbost; Donald MacMillan, 6 Crossbost. Trial was set for 13th January, 1888.

© British Library

A croft near Balallan.

The Trial

> *"These unfortunate men had against them the eloquence of the Honourable and Learned Gentleman, the Solicitor General for Scotland, and could bring no witnesses in their defence. But in this case the Gentleman and his department received a slap in the face. They only elicited a judgment to the effect that, according to the Common Law of Scotland, it was no crime to trespass..."*
>
> Dr. Cameron, MP, Glasgow College, in the House of Commons, February 21, 1888.

> *"The people of the Highlands are perfectly well aware, that the people in the South are in full sympathy with them, and that the more prosecutions there are in the High Court of Justiciary the better it would be for the Highlands and the worse for the landlords... The movement with which I have identified has found its sanction in the popular conscience. The movement is as popular in the cities as it is in the country."*
>
> Donald MacRae, Balallan, speaking in Edinburgh after the Trial of the Park deer raiders.

The six prisoners left Stornoway on the mailboat the *Locheil* on the 13th January, accompanied by witnesses for both sides. The accused men had asked the Scottish Office for assistance in calling witnesses to Edinburgh. In particular, they wanted Sheriff Fraser and the others who held 'high positions' in the island to give evidence on their behalf, but this was refused. A large crowd had gathered on the pier to give their good wishes and at various stations on the way south to the capital they were cheered by local Land League members. On arriving in Edinburgh, Rev. William MacDonald of St Columba's Free Church, Mr Donald Cowan and others met the raiders and took them to the Buchanan Hotel. That same evening the Edinburgh South Liberal Association met to discuss the land issue and the Park raid in particular. (22) It emerged at the meeting that eminent Scottish Counsel had refused to accept the brief to defend the crofters, an action which was roundly condemned by the Association.

On the following morning the trial opened to a packed court-room. On the Bench were Lord Justice Clerk Moncrieff, Lords MacLaren and Lee. The Solicitor General, Mr J.P.B. Robertson assisted by Advocates Rankine and Wallace conducted the prosecution. For the defence Donald Shaw — a long standing legal friend of the crofters — acted for Donald MacRae and Malcolm MacKenzie, Mr Macphail for

The trial of the Lewis Deer Raiders at Edinburgh.

Donald MacMillan and Roderick MacKenzie, and Mr Watt acted for John Matheson of Gravir. To *The Scotsman*, Donald MacRae was "intelligent" in appearance and well dressed with a city look. Roderick MacKenzie was a burly Highlander with broad shoulders and a bushy beard. The others were typical west coast cottars, fairly well dressed in tweeds.

The imperative for the Crown was to pin charges of mobbing and rioting and breaking the Day Trespass Act on the six. The latter charge involved establishing that they had gathered together for a common purpose specified as illegal; namely the pursuit of game. While trespass constituted grounds for damage under the Common Law, it was only a crime in instances specified under an Act of Parliament, such as the pursuit of game. Thus the men's presence in the Park deer forest was not in itself sufficient to establish that trespass had occurred.

The men were charged with "having formed a scheme that the persons living in the neighbourhood of the forest of Park should, in large numbers and armed with guns, trespass in the said forest and destroy the deer therein; and that you the said Donald MacRae, Roderick MacKenzie and John Matheson having at a meeting held on the 11th November instigated and incited persons there assembled to form part of a riotous mob for the purpose of carrying out the said scheme." (23) The charges also included intimidation of the Eishken employees.

Murdo MacRae and four other Eishken ghillies were the first Crown witnesses. Mr MacRae said there were too many men in the forest to stop, so the ghillies had concentrated on driving the deer out of firing range. He couldn't put a number on deer killed, but said the estate employees were still finding deer carcasses throughout the area. Donald MacKinnon, Balallan, was called as the sixth Crown witness. He had participated in the raid, and the case for the Prosecution hinged on his evidence.

Donald MacKinnon had turned Crown witness after all the charges against him were dropped. It transpired in the cross questioning that while in the forest MacKinnon had threatened to shoot Sheriff Fraser and Superintendent John Gordon. This was an act of great stupidity for which he would, normally, have been imprisoned. MacKinnon was the only raider who had threatened violence, he was also one of the ringleaders of the raid. Yet the Balallan man was a Tory and a member of the Primrose League, a Tory organisation whose local president was Lady Matheson.

It may be that MacKinnon infiltrated the local branch of the Land League from the outset to gather information, or he may have been told — during his time in the Stornoway jail — that by going to the Primrose League and turning Crown witness he could avoid a potentially very serious charge. Either way, he went to a gathering of the Primrose League and confessed his own crime and named a good many of the other raiders. He then struck a deal with the Stornoway authorities. They made him a free man and withdrew the charges against him. In return he was to incriminate MacRae and the others. MacKinnon told the Court that MacRae had given him money to buy half a pound of gunpowder and to obtain licences for two guns. MacKinnon also maintained that half a boll of meal was sent to his home after carrying out MacRae's instructions.

Donald Shaw, defending MacRae and MacKenzie, said it was MacKinnon who should be in the dock. "This informer himself shot the deer and tried to shoot Superintendent Gordon. That much was admitted by the man... He was cast into prison on the twofold charge of taking part in the raid and threatening to take away human life, but after he remained in prison for two days something happened. He went to Stornoway Castle on the business of the Primrose League and from that moment on the clouds were cast from his horizon, and he was in the land of prosperity. No jury on earth would rely on what he said." (24)

Hector Montgomery was the first of the five defence witnesses to be called. He testified that MacRae had advised caution, and that MacKinnon, the Crown witness, had been one of the ringleaders. The November meeting had been called, he said, to prepare the crofters' case for the Crofters Commission and to raise money for a legal representation before it. All of the subsequent evidence for the defence was along these lines. As far as the charges against the schoolmaster were concerned, Alexander MacFarlane, Marvig added that "to go after deer" was a matter they had been speaking of for some time, long before MacRae came to the district.

But it was MacRae's scalp the Crown was after. In his summing up the Solicitor General said: "MacRae's case is distinguished from the others by reason of his being a person occupying a responsible position, a man of education who was proved to be active in the affairs of the district. At one time, with great boldness and latterly with something else than boldness — with astuteness — MacRae kept himself in quiet waters while pulling the strings and sending these men out to meet their fate."

The jury took just half an hour to return verdicts of "not guilty as libelled" on all charges. They decided that no law of trespass had been broken, since the incursion was not in pursuit of breaches of the law. The judge facilitated this conclusion by determining that deer were not game, so that the raiders could not have been "in pursuit of game." The jury further decided that the events which had transpired did not constitute "mobbing and rioting."

The verdicts were received with "loud and prolonged applause in the court." Outside in the square a jubilant crowd lifted Donald MacRae shoulder-high and carried him down the High Street. The crowd halted for a moment outside *The Scotsman* offices in Cockburn Street, "during which a hostile manifestation of feeling was displayed on the part of the crowd," towards the beleaguered paper, whose correspondent in Lewis had given evidence against the raiders.

When they reached the steps of St Giles, MacRae thanked the crowd, "on behalf of the people of Lewis and on behalf of the radicals of Scotland from the bottom of my heart." He said the trial and their defence had cost them nothing and added: "We were defended by advocates and by agents who would have done credit in any area of Scottish history, and the result was proof of their ability and devotedness." That evening the raiders were entertained at The Prince of Wales hotel and travelled through to Glasgow the following morning.

© Collection of Angus Macleod

Donald MacRae, a native of Easter Ross, provided the Lochs crofters with crucial leadership in their stand against the estate.

Rev. Donald MacCallum unveiling the dedication to Donald MacRae, at the Western Necropolis, Glasgow, 1924.

The memorial stone reads: "Erected by fellow Highlanders at home and abroad as a tribute of respect to the memory of Donald MacRae, 'Balallan'. Born Plockton, February, 1851, and died Glasgow, February, 1924. One who sacrificed the best years of his life in the course of Land Law Reform and the emancipation of the oppressed and landless Highland crofters and cottars.
A man who had the courage of a chieftain, the mind of a statesman, the heart of a patriot and faith of a Christian."

The Aftermath

"I advise you to emigrate to new countries, where you can get lands cheap, and send your sons to the army and navy... I have received a splendid letter from America asking me to advise the people to go there and that they would get rich."

"The land under sheep and deer is my property and I can do with it what I like."

Lady Matheson at an interview with a delegation from
Borve, Barvas and Shader, January 3rd, 1888.

"I think the conduct of Lady Matheson must awaken the indignation of all high-minded women. She meets her starving tenants with a sneer and her splendid letter from America.

"Your only remedy is to banish them to America, where your ears can no longer be importuned by their complaints of starvation and woe. It has been the policy hitherto to banish the wailing multitudes from their stony patch of potatoes in Connemara, and their miserable townships in the Highlands. But the world is awakening slowly to the fact that to banish a population in order to satisfy the selfishness of an individual is not the remedy we ask for, nor one that justice can give."

Mrs Cunningham-Graham, Gartmore, in a letter to the
North British Daily Mail, January 9th, 1888

The Park raid sparked off a period of intense bitterness in Lewis. All over the island crofters, cottars and squatters took action to challenge the landlords' hold over them. The people of Point rioted a few days after the arrest of the Park raiders. The crofters of Borve, Shader and Barvas, about three hundred in number marched to the Lews Castle to petition Lady Matheson for the land of Galson Farm and part of the Barvas Glebe. The proprietrix turned down the request. "You should pay the rents. I pay rates and you don't pay me any rent," she complained.

From Tolsta Chaolais, Callanish and Breasclete two hundred people marched with flags flying and melodeons playing to Linshader farm in Uig. One hundred men and women marched from Tong and Aird with a petition which read: "Praying her Ladyship to restore to us our ancient boundaries so that ourselves and our families may be saved from the threatened degradation of pauperism and want..." At the same time, in Ness, *HMS Seahorse* deposited fifty Royal Marines and a contingent of Royal Scots, armed with thirty rounds of ball cartridges and provisions for two days, to arrest five men, for raiding Galson Farm and attacking the police.

Rivers which had been re-directed to improve the salmon fishings were returned to their original channels, miles of dykes were flattened, farmland was cleared of stock. All over the island people began to stake out their claim to the land by marking out lots ready for cultivation in the Spring. In Uig the Breanish crofters pledged to cultivate the cleared village of Carnish in the Spring of '88, and the Valtos and Kneep cottars kept up their long-standing pressure to occupy the farms at Reef and Timsgarry. Crofters portioned out lots at North Dell farm, and yards of dykes were pulled to the ground at Dalbeg.

For the people of Park, the victory in court had not changed anything on the ground. Their struggle for land also continued, and within a few months the forest was raided once more. The Gravir branch of the Land League met in April and resolved to proceed to Orisaigh with their spades to "turn over the ground." One hundred and fifty people marched again from Balallan to petition the proprietrix. Their poverty, she said was their own doing, and sent them on their way. The following month they re-entered the forest and pledged to "abolish sport and exterminate game in Lewis."

In the last decade of the 19th century Park deer forest was raided for a third time. (25) In March 1891, eighteen men left the overcrowded townships of Gravir, Calbost and Crossbost to settle in Orisaigh and Stiomrabhaigh and began to secure the walls and roofing of the ruined homes which had lain deserted since the clearance fifty years earlier. The men stayed there for up to three weeks, tilling the ground during the week and heading off on Friday or Saturday, either directly to their own villages or to Stornoway for provisions. They attended Church on Sundays, and went back to the settlements at the start of the following week.

On April 10th the men appeared before the Sheriff in Stornoway, interim interdicts having been served on them about a week after the start of the raid. The reasons for these raids were exactly the same as those which had pushed the landless people of Lochs into the forest four years previously. Nine of the men were admonished of having agreed to give an undertaking not to return to the forest. The remaining twelve refused to give such a promise and were sentenced to fourteen days imprisonment to be served in Inverness Jail.

On their release the Highland Land League honoured the men with a marvellous welcome. As they left the prison gates, each was presented with a pipe and supply of tobacco. Thus equipped they took their seats on a brake, which, reported the *Highland News:* "With a spanking pair of horses and a piper was in waiting, and from which was unfurled a banner bearing the legend — 'The Land for the People'."

Rev. Charles MacEachern, minister at the Established Gaelic Church Inverness and one of the early promoters of the Land League, gave an inspiring address to the gathering. Much, he said, had been achieved. Parliament had sent a Commission to the Highlands. He told the men of Lochs: "You have to be thanked for what would never have been granted but for your efforts in the cause of truth and justice — (applause). Every concession made has been silent testimony to the righteousness of your cause. But much, very much, remains to be done." (hear, hear and applause).

And MacEachern summed up the hypocrisy of the landlords' perennial case in a few brilliant lines: "But, says the representative of land interest, 'The land is valueless.' Then why occupy it? Why displace those who would make it valuable? And why persecute and imprison those who would make it valuable? What we say is what Cromwell said to a like-minded class: 'Give place to honester men'." (26)

General view of Laxay, Lochs District.

Notes and References

1. *The Scotsman*, September 25th, 1887.

2. Donald MacRae, the Balallan schoolmaster, was a native of Plockton, he served his apprenticeship in Plockton Free Church School and took a first-class Queen's Scholarship in Glasgow Free Church Training College. He was teacher of maths at Inverness Academy before taking up the post of Headmaster at Roskeen. His involvement in the issue which became known as the Roskeen case and other Land League activities led to his dismissal from the school.

3. S.R.O. AF67 / 35 all of the information about the Park Raid is contained in this file.

4. J.B. Caird, *Park:A Geographical Study of Lewis Crofting District*, 1958. See also Royal Commission (Highlands and Islands, 1892), *Report and Minutes of Evidence*, 1895, XXXVIII-XXXIX.

5. J. Munro MacKenzie, *Diary 1851*, Stornoway, 1994.

6. *Royal Commission on the Highlands and Islands, 1883, (Napier Commission)*. Evidence of John Smith, Balallan.

7. James Hunter, *The Making of the Crofting Community*, Edinburgh, 1976.

8. *Report to the Scottish Secretary*, by John Cheyne, Chief Constable for Ross-Shire. S.R.O. AF67 / 35. In December 1887 Cheyne requested a Government inquiry into the destitution which prevailed in Lewis particularly amongst the landless population.

9. Royal Commission (Highlands and Islands, 1892) *Report and Minutes of Evidence*, 1895, XXXVIII-XXXIX. Also known as the *Deer Forest Commission*.

10. Ibid.

11. Ibid.

12. *The Glasgow Herald,* November 29th and December 14th, 1887; *North British Daily Mail,* November 28th, 1887.

13. Park Trial reports in the major Scottish Newspapers.

14. S.R.O. AF67 / 35.

15. Ibid.

16. Press reports contained in S.R.O. AF67 /35.

17. S.R.O. AF67 / 35.

18. S.R.O. AF67 / 35.

19. *The Glasgow Herald*, December 1st, 1887.

20. Ibid.

21. S.R.O. AF67 / 35.

22. *The Scotsman,* January 13th, 1888.

23. Ibid., detailed reports of the trial also appear in *The Glasgow Herald* and in the *North British Daily Mail.*

24. Ibid.

25. S.R.O. AF67 / 48 deals with the subsequent raiding at Park.

26. *Highland News,* May, 1891.

3 Aignish 1888: The Struggle Intensifies

"...that on the 9th of January, all able-bodied men in the parish should gather in the same place, and march in a body to the farms of Melbost and Aignish, driving the whole stock on these farms before them towards Stornoway and on to Castle policies where they are to be left... after the stock is cleared, operations should then be commenced for preparing the soil for cultivation."

Resolution at a meeting of crofters and cottars, from the district of Point, in Garrabost Free Church, December 28th, 1887.

"Mob at Aignish, this day, large, excited and determined. Thirteen prisoners captured. Soldiers and Constables pelted with stones... I think additional force of military necessary..."

Telegraph to Lord Lothian, Secretary of State for Scotland, from Sheriff Fraser in Stornoway, January 10th, 1888.

"... I will say that a more persistent and determined attack upon the law has not been made in the history of this country..."

J.A. MacDonald, the Lord Advocate, speaking on the Aignish raid during debate on the Queen's Speech, February 21st, 1888.

On New Year's Day 1888 police constables Cameron and MacKay were instructed to keep watch at Aignish, in the district of Point, about five miles east of Stornoway. The police had word that preparations for the planned raid were about to start. Around midnight, three men appeared from the direction of Stornoway and set about demolishing the farm dykes. *The Scotsman* reporter, who had also been tipped off, hid in the byre along with the officers. He wrote: "Before they had proceeded far with their nefarious work the two officers were upon them. Two of the men escaped and ran off towards Garrabost. The other constable stuck bravely to his man, who was identified as Murdo MacDonald, Lower Bayble." The three men managed to destroy 300 yards of fencing. (1)

After MacDonald's arrest an angry crowd gathered at the farmhouse and threatened to burn the entire steading unless the man was freed. Samuel Albany Newhall, the Aignish tenant - "equal to the occasion" reported *The Scotsman* - set his gun on them. He did not shoot, but warned that the first man to come forward

NOTICE.

WHEREAS it has come to the knowledge of the Authorities that an illegal attempt is, on an early day, to be made by a mob of people to drive the Stock off Aignish Farm, in the Parish of Stornoway, and to take possession of said Farm: NOTICE IS HEREBY GIVEN, that any assemblages, for such or any similar purposes are illegal and criminal, and that all persons taking part in them, even although they individually commit no act of violence, will be guilty of the crime of mobbing and rioting, and liable to be punished therefor. AND NOTICE IS FURTHER GIVEN, that such assemblages are hereby forbidden; that on the assembly of any such riotous and disorderly persons, a Proclamation in terms of the Riot Act, and to the following effect, will be made: — "Our Sovereign Lady, the Queen, "chargeth and commandeth all persons being assembled, imme- "diately to disperse themselves, and peaceably to depart to their "habitations or to their lawful business, upon the pains contained "in the Act made in the first year of King George, for preventing "tumults and riotous assemblies." "God save the Queen;" and that if any such assemblage shall not disperse within one hour after such Proclamation, each person comprising it will be guilty of the said crime, and will be liable to the severe punishment ordered by said Act.

BY ORDER OF THE SHERIFF.

CHARLES INNES,
Sheriff-Clerk of Ross-shire.

Dingwall, 2nd January, 1888.

The Riot Act.

would do so at the risk of his own life. Newhall said he was determined to protect his house and its occupants at all costs. The crowd kept its distance, but maintained a rowdy vigil outside the farmhouse for many hours, before returning home.

Every night thereafter until the day of the raid, the crofters returned to the farmhouse to pull down the fences. A number of men surrounded the house while the others demolished the fencing. In a report which he sent to the Secretary of State for Scotland Superintendent James Gordon said the people were so enraged at the arrest of Murdo MacDonald that they turned out in force, "in order to oppose any other attempt in that direction." (2)

The bitter exchanges between Newhall and the crofters on New Year's Day and on two other occasions in the previous month were indicative of the mood of the people, and a foretaste of things to come culminating in the raid planned for January 9th. Land League meetings throughout the Point villages had established a consensus for action, which many believed was long overdue. At two crucial meetings, on December 24th and 28th at Garrabost Free Church, the Point crofters complained bitterly of their poverty and decided it was time to break the stranglehold of the landlord and his tenant farmers over their lives. (3)

They planned to raid the farms of Aignish and Melbost and take possession of the land. There was also outrage among the crofters, over the apparent misuse of the burial ground at the Aoidh (Ui) church. The crofters claimed that Newhall habitually allowed his stock to wander into the church grounds and decided to seek legal advice on any possible recourse against the farmer for the damage caused by his stock.

After the two meetings Newhall and the Melbost tenant were approached by several hundred men and women, carrying flags and banners, and asked to clear their stock. Newhall was given two weeks to vacate the farm; if he failed to do so Aignish was to be taken by force. The people were defiant, and desperate to end their poverty. They had no land to speak of and for the past two seasons the fishing had failed, their only hope of survival on the island was to cultivate the farmlands. Their pleadings made little impression upon the farmers. Samuel Newhall told the deputation they would have to reckon with a force far greater than him on the appointed day. (4)

In a telegram to the Marquis of Lothian, on January 3rd, Sheriff Fraser outlined their plans to counter the raid. Both he and the Procurator Fiscal, John Ross, would accompany the forces and police to Aignish and Melbost, in readiness for the events of the 9th. In the meantime, the Riot Act had been translated into Gaelic and was being circulated throughout the district. Subsequently, each of these notices was torn down, and one merchant had his window broken for displaying the Act. (5)

Even at this stage, less than two months after the Park raid and a few days before the planned raid at Aignish, and after months of very public discontent on the part of the crofters, the Sheriff appears to have seriously underestimated the mood of most people. He told the Secretary of State for Scotland: "I do not anticipate that any serious attempt will be made to interfere with the stock on the farm, or that we shall have much to do beyond present ourselves." (6) However, while sending out that soothing message, Sheriff Fraser clearly decided to hedge his bets, and prepared for the worst possible scenario.

At Fraser's instigation, a substantial force was assembled to represent the interests of law and order, and to stop the Point crofters in their tracks. It is difficult to ascertain whether the crofters expected the full force of the Marines and the Royal Scots to be pulled in to quell their revolt. Certainly, they anticipated that some of the raiders would be arrested. In the weeks leading up to the raid, the press carried interviews with crofters who declared that they were prepared to face a term in jail on the grounds that jail would be an improvement on the poverty they faced from day to day as free men.

Eighty Marines and Royal Scots were put at Sheriff Fraser's disposal. He already had 18 constables; his entire complement were to be deployed at Aignish, in spite of outbreaks of lawlessness in other parts of the island. On Sunday 8th January, before daybreak, the police were marched to Aignish where they received orders to attract as little attention as possible, and to get under cover around the farm buildings. Both the Sheriff and the Procurator Fiscal were with the force. The authorities were determined to resist the raid and prepared accordingly.

In the small hours of Monday morning, the *HMS Seahorse* landed the Marines in Sandwick Bay, under the command of Captain Plumb and Lieutenant Bradley. They set off across the fields avoiding the main road. "The march under the narrow crescent of the moon was comfortably made," reported *The Scotsman* in full war correspondent style. Another detachment of Royal Marines was sent out to Melbost.

At Aignish, the whole force was kept out of sight, under cover of the farm buildings. Rumour had it that the crofters would bide their time, until they were certain the coast was clear. But this proved false. The crofters appeared as planned at 11a.m. From the farmhouse they could be seen against the skyline, gathering quickly for the march from the village to the farmhouse. In only a matter of minutes several hundred men and women had congregated. Some carried sticks and bludgeons. They shouted and whistled, and for a little while it seemed to those who awaited them at the farmhouse that things would go no further. (7)

Within minutes, the crowd swelled to around 400 and suddenly the action began. The raiders scattered all over the farm, driving the cattle and ponies down to low ground. Sheriff Fraser, Superintendent Gordon and the Procurator Fiscal decided it was time to intervene. Escorted by a couple of policemen they began to walk towards the crofters, and asked them, in Gaelic, to disperse peaceably. But each time he tried to pacify the crowd, they shouted: "Our families are starving. We need the land." (8)

From his vantage point at the Aignish farmhouse, *The Scotsman* correspondent reported: "Scores of crofters might now be seen hurrying down the fields from the Knock direction, to join the raiders, who were scattered over several fields and

Reading the Riot Act at Aignish Farm, near Stornoway.

presented a memorable spectacle." (9) The upper fields were quickly cleared of all stock and the raiders made their way to the low-lying areas adjacent to the farmhouse where several hundred sheep were grazing. They were driven off in the Stornoway direction along with the rest of the stock. The police, who had remained under cover at the farm steading, were only then ordered out. Shortly afterwards the Marines emerged from the buildings at the double, with bayonets fixed.

By mid-day up to 1,000 people were scattered throughout the farmlands, oblivious to the Marines' presence. The incredulous *Scotsman* reporter wrote: "They simply did not pay any attention to the Marines ... and were not in the least deterred from the chase... They did not desist until every hoof had been driven out at the other end of the farm, and up the brae of Sandwick and beyond." (10)

Ultimately the cattle driving was left to a "few score" of people. The remainder were behind the farm steadings fleeing from Sheriff Fraser and his men who had adopted a policy of giving chase in order to arrest as many of the raiders as they could lay hands on. A clash between the crowd and the military was inevitable, and when it happened the *Scotsman* correspondent was on the spot and able to give a meticulous account of the event:

"The marines, running across the fields, intercepted the people at the entrance of the narrow isthmus connecting Point to Stornoway. They were then halted at the opposite side of the farm, at a place where the public road to Point runs between banks that are five feet in height. They were drawn up in two ranks on the barn side of the road. The crofters mustered on the other side, extending a deep form along the face of the bank. Immediately behind them, down a steep bank was the beach, where the sea, open to a South West wind was being driven up in great rollers." (11)

In the meantime the police were making heavy weather of the arrests. "Here and there a policeman might be seen in grips with a crofter, who was making the best effort to wrench himself away from the grasps of the law; and sometimes it took two or three policemen to make one arrest," *The Scotsman* related. (12) Ten men were captured by the police, they were handcuffed and taken alongside the line of Marines. Around seven hundred people, tired and angry, now gathered face to face with the perceived servants of their oppressors, the military and police who were assembled on the opposite side of the bank. The crowd shouted and brandished their sticks. The raid was not yet over until the arrested men were set free.

The bitterness was intense, as the two sides faced each other with open contempt. Young men jeered and challenged the soldiers to fight without their weapons. Moments later a few of them jumped onto the road. The police, seizing the opportunity to make further arrests, leapt amongst the men, but only managed to collar one of them.

This only served to provoke the raiders, and the crowd surged forward to rescue the man. "A score of sticks were swung about the heads of the policemen who tried

Police and Marines seizing the riotous crofters.

to drag their prisoner up the dyke. Mr Ross, the Procurator Fiscal, leaned over to give the police a hand. He was attacked and received three or four severe blows on the head and neck with a bludgeon." (13) In a potentially disastrous move Ross, who was also Lady Matheson's lawyer, produced a revolver. It was an act of gross stupidity which greatly heightened the feeling of the crowd. The level headed Sheriff Fraser calmed the crowd, urging reason and restraint. Ross returned the revolver into the holster, but the mayhem continued.

A number of Marines next went to the aid of the police, leaping down to surround the constables and the arrested man. They then fixed their bayonets and turned to face the crowd, in order to keep it at bay. But the apparent success of the police in securing the man's detention only added to the fury. Disregarding the fixed bayonets the crowd pushed forward and tried to get at the Marines. Some of the younger boys began to pelt the soldiers with stones and clods of earth. Sensing the increased danger of outright and bloody violence, their commanding officer ordered the troops back to their original positions. Sheriff Fraser and Superintendent Gordon remained amongst the rioters, trying to defuse the situation. But the incensed crowd continued to demand the release of the arrested men. Sheriff Fraser finally read the Riot Act and explained its provisions in Gaelic. It was greeted with derision. The crowd were only interested in retrieving the arrested raiders, and were prepared, if necessary, to follow the men to Stornoway.

A Marine captain set off to Melbost in order to summon the support of the Royal Scots who were posted there. They were to accompany the prisoners to the jail in Stornoway. *The Scotsman* reported: "The delay gave the crowd time to cool. Superintendent Gordon, while their feelings were hottest, kept his place, going among the people and advising them to go off. The Sheriff also from time to time exerted himself in the same direction, and at other times could be seen going about in front of the crowd calmly smoking his pipe." (14)

One of the arrested men, older than the others, tried to persuade the crowd to disperse. "Go home," he said. "Go home to the children and look after them." (15) Nobody paid any attention. A crowd of women, some of whom had participated in the raid, gathered on the slopes of the adjoining village to demonstrate their support. Others arrived from the town and the outlying villages to cheer the raiders. Remarkably, the whole affair only lasted a little over two hours. The Royal Scots arrived shortly after one o'clock to remove the arrested men to the jail. The procession moved off, with the police and prisoners in the centre, surrounded on all sides by the soldiers.

As they marched off the crowd hurled clods of earth, stones and their sticks at the retreating column. After a while, the people dispersed and headed for home, bringing to an end one of the bitterest and most violent confrontations in crofting history.

The Background

"...but, still, there was something to explain their conduct ... the explanation is simple —the despair of the people..."

Dr. R MacDonald MP (Ross and Cromarty),
during debate on the Queen's Speech, February 21st, 1888.

"...we are so depressed that the fear of the estate management and the like of that has taken the courage out of us."

Kenneth MacLeod, Garrabost, in his evidence
to the Napier Commission, 1883.

Aignish was a Tack long before the events of 1888. In the Seaforth era the subtenant at Aignish would have had small tenantry on the farm, but by the time Matheson bought the island in 1844 Aignish was in the hands of a single tenant, a Mr Alexander, who worked the farm in the middle years of the century, before the lease fell to the Newhalls in the 1870s. Samuel Albany Newhall succeeded his father as lessee and had held the lease for four years prior to the raid. When Newhall gave evidence at the raiders' trial he said Aignish was a grazing farm, but that was not always the case.

When Alexander held the lease Aignish was a well-cultivated arable farm. Torcuil MacLeod of Garrabost in his evidence to the Napier Commission in 1883 said of Aignish: "I remember the tack adjoining our township having been occupied by a crofting population. I could buy a stone of meal there when I required it, a barrel of potatoes, a bushel of oats and a pint of milk. I see nothing on that farm today except green grass, rushes and white sheep..." (16) Alexander's farming methods came under scrutiny when Matheson bought the island, and it is likely that early in the Matheson proprietorship Aignish was targeted for the increasingly lucrative pursuit of sheep farming. (17)

Aignish was extended over the decade by the gradual addition of land which had been held for generations by the crofting population. Machair land, a portion of arable and moor grazings were taken by Matheson's estate from the people of Knock and added to Aignish. Another piece of good arable was lost to the estate, to form the glebe of the Established Church. Additional charges were laid on those crofters who wanted the use of their former pasture lands — two shillings for a piece of summer pasture for one cow, 4d for a sheep.

In the village of Garrabost, hill pasture had been removed when a brick and tile works was established in 1850. Cattle and horses were poinded if they wandered onto its grounds and the peat banks were also taken over by the tile works. The works represented a classic example of Sir James Matheson's 'work schemes', established in the immediate post-famine years.

When these failed Matheson's factor John Munro Mackenzie toured the villages telling the crofters that "if they remained they need not look to the proprietor for relief in food, seed, corn or employment, and that they would be expected to pay up their rent on the term day, otherwise they would be deprived of their buildings." (18) Although there were still no volunteers for emigration, a number from each village who were to be compulsorily removed was fixed by the factor.

A similarly harsh regime continued to be operated by Munro MacKenzie's successor, Donald Munro. This was the reality of relationships between the crofters and estate which was reflected in the evidence to the Napier Commission, and which created the mood of bitterness and desperation which persisted as the times grew harder, in the late 1880s.

Point was one of the great fishing areas of Lewis. The people tried desperately to survive by the fishing, and although they did incredibly well against the odds, it was a fierce existence. The boats were poor; pier and landing facilities ranged from grossly inadequate to nonexistent. Between 1860 and 1886 there were six drowning tragedies in the district. In each case all of the crew was lost, usually six men, and very often they were of the same family. With the sons lost there were only the widows and the older people left to raise young families. John Stewart of Bayble told the Napier Commission: "My own son, along with four of a crew, was drowned by the capsizing of the boat at our own door ... our only resource (was) in this way cut away from us..." (19) In 1882, severe weather destroyed seven fishing boats belonging to the village of Knock — the place where the boats were tied up did not provide sufficient shelter against the wild October gales.

In the main churchyard of the Ui, the inscription on one grave stone reads: "Erected by D. MacDonald R.N., Portnaguran, in memory of his dear parents, D. MacDonald drowned 14th January, 1881 aged 28 years; Jessie Ferguson MacDonald, died 20th October, aged 30 years, and uncles Malcolm and Norman Ferguson drowned 14th January, 1881, aged 22 and 20 years respectively." (20) It is an eloquent indictment of the conditions under which these people struggled to live and work. Kenneth MacLeod of Garrabost told the Napier Commission in 1883: "Although the loss of life and property from want of proper harbour accommodation had been considerable, we got no help or encouragement from the estate for making a harbour; and a quay which was made at Bayble, by a stranger with the help of fishermen, who contributed £1 per crew, was destroyed, the stones having been removed for making improvements connected with the estate." (21) Never once was there an offer of help, never once was the hand of kindness or charity extended from the Matheson estate. Their only contribution to the lives of these people was to hinder progress and to extract as much as possible in rent.

When the villages were lotted in the 1850s the land available to crofters was greatly reduced. For instance, eight crofting families lived in Aird before the Matheson proprietorship; in 1883, 34 families lived in the village, sixteen of them with crofts and the remainder as squatters. The eight former crofts were sub-divided and the pasture land was added to the inbye land to create the additional crofts. The inevitable result was over-crowding and impoverishment. In Upper Bayble there were originally 24 crofts, but by the 1880s there were 103 families trying to eke out meagre livings in the village. By then all the inbye land was used for lots. The lack of pasture land meant people could not have any stock, because of the congestion the old arable land was being exhausted. There was no other land on which to raise crops.

When, against this background of impoverishment, the crofters' conflict in the late eighties brought with it large-scale media attention, reporters from the Scottish newspapers visited the Point townships as they had done a few months previously in Park. *The Glasgow Herald* reported a "widespread appearance of poverty." In the village of Aird, the paper's correspondent found a "preponderance of the cottar element ... squatters with no land, mostly fishermen, but the failure of the fishing in the past two seasons has brought a great deal of hardship — they are deeply involved with the meal merchants." (22)

In the house of Malcolm MacKenzie, they found a family of six young children. There was no meal in the house; only a small supply of potatoes. MacKenzie had a fifth share in a fishing boat and in common with others in the village relied on income from local and east coast fishing. In each one of the homes visited the story was the same, though some of the houses were very poor and others were "comfortable and well built." Irrespective of previous circumstances, they were now dependent upon the good-will of the merchants and particularly on Torcuil MacLeod, the Garrabost merchant who was a "popular man amongst the crofters." (23)

It was these conditions of poverty which led directly to the events at Aignish. For decades, the people had suffered reductions in the land to which they had access. They had suffered the affront of seeing prosperous farmers operating much of that land as a single farm. They had suffered manifold injustices at the hands of an autocratic landowner and his factors. All of this could be borne, as long as the fishing and general economy were good enough to provide the means of modest livelihoods. But by the late 1880s, the oppression of circumstances had closed in on the crofters and finally forced their emotions to the surface. The time was now overdue to restore the land to the people who were so much in need of it.

The Trial

> "Alexander MacLeod, first witness for the defence, twice expressed his desire to speak in Gaelic, but Lord Craighill refused... As MacLeod was about to leave the box, the judge said they were all much obliged to him for speaking English which he was so well able to do. He should never speak Gaelic when he could speak English, except among his friends."
>
> Account of the first part of the Aignish Raiders' Trial,
The Scotsman, January 31st, 1888.

With the Aignish prisoners in custody, a telegram from the Scottish Office in Dover House to the Admiralty called for immediate naval assistance to back up the forces already on Lewis. The *HMS Belleisle*, anchored at Portree, received word to collect 60 marines and proceed to Stornoway forthwith. Two days later, on January 12th, thirteen Aignish prisoners were dispatched to Dingwall. The forces of law and order had decided that it was "dangerous" to hold the men in the town jail. (24)

Rumours of a rescue attempt to free the Aignish raiders prompted the move from Stornoway for "sure-keeping." The prisoners were removed from their cells at 2 a.m. — the whole affair was conducted with great secrecy. The men went to bed at the usual time; after a while the police were ordered into the Sheriff Court building in twos and threes. The detachment of Royal Scots, stationed at Manor Farm, was brought down to form an escort. After these preparations were complete, the prisoners were aroused, taken out into the courtyard and handcuffed. (25)

Among those on the spot was the *Scotsman* correspondent, who followed the procession down to the pier: "Guarded by a strong cordon of police, and with the Royal Scots in the front and rear, the rear guard with fixed bayonets, they were marched quickly to the pier ... the streets were silent and empty but for the steady tramping of the men, and there was not a light but that of the stars." The men were put on board the *HMS Jackal* which proceeded immediately to Stromeferry. They were taken to Dingwall by train and marched, still handcuffed to the town jail. The men were reported to be 'quite unconcerned' (26) about their fate and although poorly clad were well and healthy.

The prisoners spent ten days at Dingwall, with one allowed out on bail to arrange their defence. Four warders from the Calton jail in Edinburgh were sent to Dingwall to accompany the men to the capital for the trial, which had been fixed for January 30th. Two Lewis men, Rev. Mr MacAskill, and Mr Morrison, a school teacher in the town, saw the prisoners off at Dingwall station. The men were detained in the Calton jail until the day of the trial.

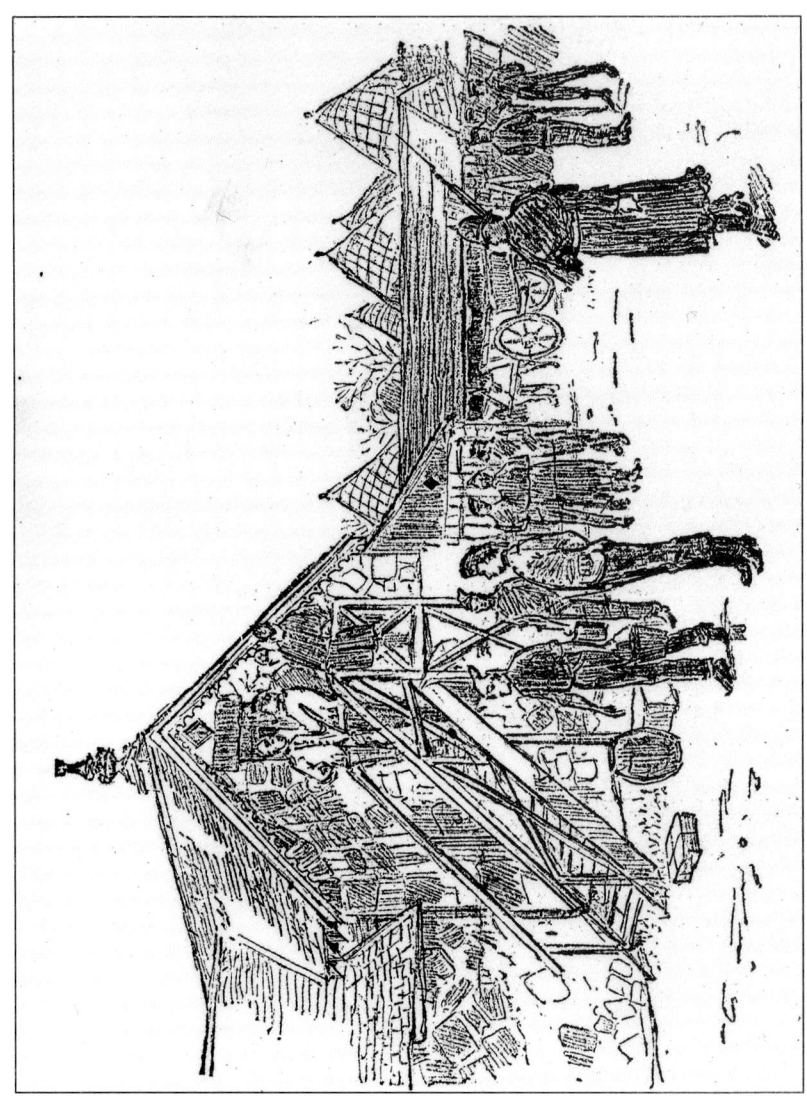

Manor Farm, Stornoway, the quarters of the Royal Scots.

The Scottish Office, still reeling with disbelief after the acquittal of the Park raiders, was determined that on this occasion a 'guilty' verdict would be returned. In correspondence with the Scottish Secretary, Northern Chief Constable John Cheyne said the Park verdict was "most extraordinary and disheartening" and he feared the result would "gravely increase the difficulties of the situation." (27) It was apparent from the outset that the Aignish raiders were to face a much tougher prosecution, as a second acquittal would be completely unacceptable to the authorities.

A different judge, Lord Craighill — with the reputation of being a belligerent and uncompromising hard-liner — was to preside over the Aignish trials. Lord Moncrieff was regarded as far too soft and accommodating on the 'crofters' ' question'.5 The Lord Advocate, Mr J.H.A. MacDonald QC, assisted by his depute, Mr John Rankine, personally led for the prosecution. Eight lawyers and Counsel represented the defendants and Professor MacKinnon acted as interpreter. (28)

The trial was conducted in stages with the prisoners divided into groups. It was, to say the least, an unusual arrangement, and Lord Craighill told the court that it was to take account of the large number of defendants. However, a few days after the trial had been concluded, the pro-crofter Sutherland MP, Angus Sutherland, put a different construction on the procedure when he told the House of Commons: "The only reason I can conceive for the adoption of such a course is this — if some of the prisoners were acquitted, as the deer raiders in the parish of Lochs were, another jury was to be empanelled." (29)

The thirteen men were charged with "forming part of a riotous mob — which, armed with sticks and bludgeons, and acting of common purpose, trespassed on the farm and drove off the cattle and sheep stock. They then endeavoured to rescue prisoners from the custody of the Police; having failed in their attempts, they then assaulted with stones, clods and sticks the marines, soldiers and others."

The Government had refused to meet any expenses for defence witnesses, with the result that the men's defence was poor. The few people who made it to Edinburgh did so with the help of the Crofters' Relief Fund; they were not as well informed or as well briefed as the witnesses who had appeared for the Park raiders. The entire defence was somewhat implausibly based on the claim that the people had gathered at the churchyard to examine the damage done to it. The large numbers involved — allegedly gathering at a churchyard for the sole purpose of looking over the damage done by the farmer's cattle — weakened any possible credibility which this line of defence may have carried, and the Lord Advocate was quick to mock it.

He subsequently alluded in Parliament to the crofters' weak line of defence, when challenged about the government's refusal to pay expenses of the defence witnesses: "They were to be brought down — what for? For the purpose of proving that the whole of this assemblage of 700 people — yelling and swearing and rioting — was for no other object than to visit the graves of their ancestors... The Executive

The trial of the Aignish raiders, Edinburgh.

would have made itself the laughing-stock of the whole country. Why, one of the prisoners, when he heard such evidence given in his favour, was so astonished that he went off into a perfect fit of laughter." (30)

Superintendent Gordon was the first witness for the prosecution, claiming to have seen a number of his men struck by the raiders. He told the court that the Procurator Fiscal had received three blows; that one of the accused, Alex MacLeod, had been caught by Ross and that in order to release himself MacLeod hit the Fiscal with "a blind stroke, backwards." (31)

John Mackay, the first of the raiders to be captured, was about to strike down the horse of Captain Farquharson of the Royal Scots when he was seized by the Police. Superintendent Gordon also told the court of the 'obscene expressions' in Gaelic which were shouted by the crowd when the Riot Act was finally read. There was, he said, "a shout that the Queen may go to hell." The court heard that all of the speeches at the meeting of December 24th had contained threats of violence with all of those who spoke claiming that they "would shed their blood to carry out the resolution." (32)

Samuel Albany Newhall, the Aignish lessee, said that although he had been tenant at Aignish for four years and his father some years before that he had engaged in "very little intercourse with the neighbouring crofters." He recalled that on December 24th, he had been approached by a crowd of 300 people carrying red flags, and was given fourteen days to vacate the farm. (33)

When Alexander MacLeod, the first witness for the defence, twice expressed his desire to speak Gaelic, he was met with an impatient refusal from Lord Craighill who insisted that the evidence was given in English. When the Aird fisherman Norman Campbell stood in the witness box he was also ordered to speak English. "You can speak English very well," said the judge. (34) The two men could only say in defence of the raiders that they went to the churchyard, and that the raid was not premeditated. In his summing up after the first day's proceedings the Lord Advocate proclaimed: "If mobbing and rioting are to become recognised means by which people can get what they had not, two things could happen: all property would become unsafe and all prosperity would cease and tyranny would be allowed to come in." Lord Craighill added helpfully: "This trial is one of great importance and it is in the interest of the public that there should not be a miscarriage of justice." The first three men were found guilty as libelled. (35)

The Gaelic issue was to the fore on the second day of the trial. Donald Smith of Aird simply refused to speak English; he said that he could not. He stood stolidly in the witness box with his right hand raised and apparently deaf to His Lordship's persuasions. Eventually Lord Craighill threatened: "If I come to know that you can speak and understand English, I will consider what to do in order to vindicate the offence of contempt of court." (36) The evidence followed the same pattern, and this second batch of raiders was also convicted. The next day, a third instalment followed in the same way, while the final batch were absolved only of the conditional charges of assault which were levelled against them. The precaution of trying them in groups had proven to be unnecessary. The Edinburgh jury had found guilty all 16 of the men charged as Aignish raiders.

Lord Craighill declared it to be his duty to pass heavy sentences; anything else "would not be just to the prisoners themselves or to the community." Two Aird Fishermen, Alexander MacLeod (60) and Donald MacKenzie (51) were each sentenced to 15 months. MacLeod was found guilty of striking John Ross, the Depute Procurator Fiscal. Seven of the raiders received sentences of 12 months. They were: John Mackay, William MacLeod (jun.), Colin Nicholson, Donald MacLeod, William MacLeod (sen.), Murdo MacDonald and Allan MacDonald.

One of the witnesses, Kenneth MacDonald, who was a Stornoway merchant, had said that he was standing with Allan MacDonald when he was arrested. He had been left alone because he was dressed like a gamekeeper, while Allan — dressed like a crofter — was arrested!

Three of the men were each sentenced to nine months. They were John MacLeod, Broker, Malcolm MacKenzie, and John MacLeod, Aird.

Finally, 22 year old Murdo MacDonald of Lower Bayble was jailed for six months for pulling down the farm fences. MacDonald was the only breadwinner in the home, but the judge showed no compassion.

The verdicts were posted in shop windows in Stornoway and Point. According to *The Scotsman,* the news "caused great dismay and anger amongst the people." In Glasgow, petitions were organised against the sentences. But perhaps the most eloquent and effective answer to the proceedings came from a Land League meeting in Portree. Certainly, the sentences were condemned — but the meeting also called on all crofters not to be deterred, "by the brutal inflictions of a Tory Government, and to manfully maintain the agitation in such a manner as will carry the sympathy of all patriotic and sympathetic people." (37)

The Months After the Trial

Weeks after the trial and imprisonment of the Aignish Raiders, the HMS *Seahorse* landed 40 Marines and a party of police at Bayble to assist with more arrests. The Captain of the *HMS Belleisle* wrote to the Secretary of State: "It would appear to be hardly necessary to send so large a force for the arrest of two persons, but I am assured by the Sheriff that such is the state of feeling among the populace that the police have no control and are liable to be stoned." (38)

Military assistance was, indeed, called in after two constables had been stoned. On February 27th, two policemen were on their rounds down towards Portvoller when they were attacked by a crowd of women and boys and stoned along the road for several hundred yards. A day later the same hapless policemen returned to the village to serve interdicts against two men who were suspected of pulling down fences around Aignish farm, after the raid, and again the women and children of the village set about them with stones and clods of earth. (39)

The policemen had succeeded in serving the interdicts before the crowd gathered. They left the citation in the home of Malcolm MacLeod, ignoring protests of the occupants, all of whom refused to accept it. When the officer laid the notice on the table it was taken by one of the women and thrown out the door, before they chased the retreating policemen out of the village.

It was when the time came to apprehend the men, Murdo MacKenzie and Malcolm MacLeod, that the marines were bought in. The "best and safest way" (40) to effect the apprehension was formulated by the Superintendent of Police and those military chiefs remaining on the island. The Superintendent of Police would go with eight men to Bayble on *HMS Seahorse* in order to approach the homes of the accused from the sea. The Sheriff Substitute and the Depute Procurator Fiscal were to set off overland and meet up at Bayble. *HMS Seahorse* was to lie in Bayble bay, and would only land the Marines if back up was required.

Again the women resisted attempts to remove the men at first claiming that one of them was unfit to travel the distance to Stornoway. The ship's doctor was then called, only to declare the man fit and well enough to travel! A large crowd had gathered at the houses of the accused, determined to resist the arrests, and although the Marines were called in to help the police it was eventually decided to withdraw. To avoid open confrontation the Sheriff called off his men and asked the accused to "present themselves voluntarily" at Stornoway Police Station the following day. The police and the Marines returned to the ship, jeered and shouted at by the crowd. The two men did give themselves up, and were duly committed for trial. (41)

Women played a crucial role in encouraging resistance, and took a full part in the Aignish riot although none was arrested.

The women, Marion MacLeod and Marion MacKenzie, were very much to the fore at Aignish when the farm was again raided two months later in May 1888. Seven raiders, all from Knock, succeeded in driving 50 head of cattle off the farm. After much persuasion from the police, the raiders agreed to leave the farm and there were no further arrests. (42)

Thus the events at Aignish passed into crofting history, emphasising that the passing of the 1886 Crofters Act had left much unfinished business. The people of Point had to wait a further 17 years for victory at Aignish; when, in 1905, the estate came under the proprietorship of Major Duncan Matheson, a nephew of Sir James. The farm of Aignish was divided into crofts and the first houses were occupied in the spring of that year. The tenants listed below were the first to settle on the old farmland of Aignish when the farm was returned to crofting:

1. Niall Ailein (Neil MacLeod, formerly of 17 Swordale)
2. Murchadh Uilleim Choinnich (Murdo Murray, Knock)
3. Seòras Tharmoid Iain (George MacLeod, 15 Swordale)
4. Niall Mhurchaidh Nèill (Neil MacKay, 16 Swordale)
5. Dòmhnall Chaluim Alasdair (Donald MacLeod, 5 Knock)
6. Uilleam Choinnich Alasdair (William Crichton, 27 Knock)
7. Tarmod Ruairidh Bhàin (Norman MacLeod, 29 Upper Bayble)
8. Murchadh Ruairidh Tàillear (Murdo MacKenzie, 14 Knock)
9. Iain Ruairidh Bhàin (John MacLeod, 29 Upper Bayble)
10. Iomhar MacRath (Evander MacRae, 13 Swordale)
11. Iain Choinnich Bhig (John MacKenzie, 9 Knock)
12. Calum Alasdair Bhig (Malcolm Munro, 29 Knock)
13. Iain Mhurchaidh Nèill (John MacKay, 16 Swordale)
14. Coinneach 'an Choinnich (Kenneth MacMillan, 24 Swordale)
15. Iain Alasdair Alasdair (John MacRae, 13 Swordale)
16. Uilleam Mhic Choinnich (William MacAskill, Lower Bayble)
17. Niall Barrant (Neil MacLeod, 1 Knock)
18. Murchadh Iain (Murdo MacLeod, 14 Swordale)
19. Dòmhnall Caimbeul (Donald Campbell, 26 Swordale)
20. Calum Mhurchaidh Portair (Malcolm MacDonald, 15 Shader)
21. Murchadh 'an 'ic Dhòmhnaill (Murdo MacSween, 7 Shader)
22. Dòmhnall Portair (Donald MacDonald, 10 Swordale)
23. Dòmhnall Alasdair Tàillear (Donald MacIver, 27 Swordale)
24. Iain Tharmoid 'ic Aoidh (John MacKay, 3 Swordale)
25. Dòmhnall Chaluim Mhurchaidh (Donald MacDonald, 2 Swordale)
26. Tarmod Chaluim Mhurchaidh (Norman MacDonald, 2 Swordale)
27. Iain Alasdair Bhig (John Munro, 28 Knock)

28. Calum 'an 'ic Mhurchaidh (Malcolm MacIver, 12 Swordale)
29. Daibhidh Barrant (David MacLeod, 1 Knock)
30. Aonghas 'an 'ic Mhurchaidh Mhòir (Angus MacDonald, 7 Shader)
31. Uilleam Uilleim (Willliam MacLeod, 17 Upper Shader)
32. Iain Tharmoid Iain (John MacLeod, 25 Swordale)

Notes and References

1. *The Scotsman,* December 26th, 1887.
2. Ibid.
3. The Garrabost Free Church minister the Rev. George MacLeod was present at the meeting. John Crichton, Swordale, presided until the resolution to raid was read out; he then gave up the chair so that no one person could be singled out by the authorities.
4. The family of Samuel Newhall were amongst the first entrepreneurs to develop the Harris Tweed industry; they moved into tweed production before the first war.
5. S.R.O. AF67 / 38.
6. Ibid.
7. *The Scotsman,* January 10th, 1888. The paper had its own correspondent at the scene, and he was able to give a full and detailed report of the raid.
8. Ibid.
9. Ibid.
10. Ibid.
11. Ibid. This scene is almost exactly reproduced in the illustration from *The Illustrated London News.*
12. Ibid.
13. Ibid.
14. Ibid.
15. Ibid.
16. *Royal Commission for the Highlands and Islands, 1883,* (*Napier Commission*) Evidence of Kenneth MacLeod, Garrabost and information on wages being taken in lieu of rent can be found in J. Munro MacKenzie, *Diary 1851,* Stornoway, 1994.
17. J. Munro MacKenzie, *Diary 1851,* Stornoway, 1994.
18. Ibid.

19. *Royal Commission for the Highlands and Islands, 1883, (Napier Commission)* AF50.
20. B. Lawson, *St. Columba's Church,* Stornoway.
21. *Royal Commission for the Highlands and Islands, 1883, (Napier Commission)* AF50.
22. SRO AF 83/188.
23. Ibid.
24. S.R.O. AF83 / 188.
25. *The Scotsman*, January 13th, 1888.
26. Ibid.
27. S.R.O. AF83 / 188.
28. *The Scotsman*, January 31st, 1888.
29. *Hansard,* January 31st, 1888.
30. *Hansard,* February 21st, 1888.
31. *The Scotsman*, January 31st, 1888.
32. Ibid.
33. Ibid.
34. Ibid.
35. Ibid.
36. *The Scotsman,* February 1st, 1888.
37. S.R.O. AF67 / 42.
38. SRO AF 67/42.
39. Ibid.
40. Ibid.
41. Ibid.
42. Ibid.

4 Coll and Gress

> "My own view all along has been that there is no reason why the development of small holdings and the development of Lord Leverhulme's work should clash in any way, and I have never been able to find any reasonable man who had been able to discover why they should necessarily clash."
>
> Dr. Donald Murray, House of Commons; August 4th, 1920.

> "The Lewismen are seamen mainly and this war has shown it is in the national interest they should continue as seamen. To industrialise them seems to be a questionable policy. It is necessary to look ahead and consider what effects will follow in Lewis should the population be increased by industrialisation, and then be followed by a failure in industry.."
>
> Thomas Wilson, Board of Agriculture Officer for Lewis;
> in a report to the Board, September 26th, 1918.

The years after the First World War produced in Lewis the classic conflict, in which the mighty Lord Leverhulme and his plans for industrialisation were pitted against the quite different aspirations of crofters. The rudiments of the story are well-known, but history has generally been written from the vantage point of Leverhulme and those men of commerce who supported his plans. This treatment of events had scarcely done justice to the courage or vision of his crofter adversaries, to the historical circumstances which underlay their determination, or to the arrogant intransigence of Leverhulme himself. Leverhulme did not only want to gain access to particular farms, in order to supply the needs of a newly industrialised Stornoway workforce. He was also deeply committed to the destruction of crofting tenure throughout the island of Lewis. (1)

It was due to the obstructions created by Leverhulme's predecessor as owner of Lewis that the farms which became the subject of post-war controversy, including Gress, were not already under crofting tenure. If things had gone according to plan, and the Board of Agriculture had been allowed to fulfil its commitments to the Lewis people, the large farms would have been broken up into crofts even before the commencement of hostilities in 1914. (2)

A formal application for the break-up of a number of Lewis farms, including Gress, was lodged by the Board of Agriculture with the Land Court in July 1914. (3) The process of acquisition had been initiated the previous year, but fraught negotiations between the Board and representatives of the Lewis proprietor, Major Duncan Matheson, delayed the formal applications to the Land Court. Every legal obstacle had been placed in the way of the Board. When they served the estate with statutory notice of the resettlement plan, Major Matheson interdicted the Board. The eventual application was amended "as nearly as possible, on the lines desired by the proprietor," in order to avoid litigation. (4) The Land Court heard the case in March 1915, and in the following June the Court visited Lewis to inspect the farms. Another hearing was held to consider further amendments proposed by the estate. Even at this stage, the Board were optimistic about the eventual outcome; a memo between officials suggested that there was "reason to believe that the Court will issue Affirmative Orders for Galson, Gress, Carnish and Ardroil and a Rejection Order is expected for Orinsay." (5)

Forty new holdings were to be created at Gress, varying in size from 7 to 26 acres arable, with 3,321 acres of common hill pasture. Major Matheson was to receive £2,000 in compensation while Peter Liddle, an Ayrshire man who was the Gress tenant, would get £700. The neighbouring Coll farm did not enter negotiations at this stage, since it was too small to meet the criteria (150 acres or £80 annual rental) which determined whether the Board of Agriculture could schedule the land for division. (6) However, the estate continued to prevaricate over Gress and the other farms and decided to state a Special Case to the Court of Session, "so that they may have further opportunity of vexation, opposition and litigation," reported a frustrated BOAS officer. (7)

With the country at war, the Board of Agriculture had more immediate priorities. It could not afford, and did not want, costly litigation. Instead of pursuing the matter the Board recommended "an indefinite postponement" of the resettlement schemes. The chairman, Sir Robert Greig, wrote to the Secretary of State that abandoning the scheme altogether "would be a better course if the cases were normal, but in view of the peculiar position in Lewis and the certainty that agrarian troubles would inevitably follow, the Board hesitates to recommend that course." (8) Therefore, postponement until the war was over was the option agreed upon.

Even before the end of hostilities the Board of Agriculture began preparations to relaunch the Lewis schemes "at least up to the point of having everything ready to go on with the actual execution at the end of the war." (9) In September 1917 the Board was given permission by the Secretary of State to apply to the Land Court for the recall of the sist and to issue Compulsory Orders in respect of the Lewis farms. (10) By then however a whole new dimension was introduced which was to radically alter the scenario. Duncan Matheson was in the process of selling the island to William Hesketh Lever, first Viscount Leverhulme, founder and controller of the huge industrial empire Lever Brothers. When the island passed into his hands in May 1918 Leverhulme wrote: "My object with the Isle of Lewis is not business, but to find a delightful home in a beautiful island and among a people whom I greatly admire and respect, and who will, I am certain, prove most charming friends and neighbours." (11)

None of this was the concern of the survivors from the Great War. They had fought for their country and were to be rewarded at last with land and homes to call their own. As far as they were concerned, the matter was urgent and straightforward: the schemes for the acquisition and division of land, which had been proposed should now proceed in time for the ex-servicemen to commence spring work on the new crofts. It transpired, however, that crofting was anathema to the new landlord, that he had his own very firm plans for the farms in question, and that his declared intention to refrain from business in Lewis had quickly been replaced with grand schemes of industrialisation. Fish canning was to be the principal industry, and by August 1918 he had lodged his first plans with the Ministry of Food. Enthused by his own rapidly developing plans to turn Stornoway into the Port Sunlight of the north, Leverhulme settled on the opinion that crofting was the root cause of the island's economic misery. In much the same way, a few years earlier, he had condemned traditional methods of agriculture in British West Africa and the Congo where he also held huge tracts of land. All he saw in these countries was waste, inefficiency and idleness. "Natives," he said, "should be treated as willing children; housed, doctored and moved from place to place as required. Above all they should be taught the value of regular habits and of working to time." (12) In Lewis he held crofting in the same low regard; as inefficient and economically debilitating. The people were "merely existing" and crofting was an "entirely impossible way of life." (13) Rural Lewis was the very heartland of crofting and Leverhulme realised that he could do little, in the short term at any rate, to alter that. But he soon made clear that he would do everything in his power to prevent its extension.

In the first months of his proprietorship Leverhulme travelled the length and breadth of the island. The country people asked him for peat roads and village roads, small harbours and other basic facilities which were needed to assist in the day to day organisation of crofting. Meanwhile the townspeople, and especially the middle classes, were wooed, feted and partied. (14) In the eyes of many, Leverhulme created an atmosphere of hope and trust. However, while still unaware of the specific threat posed to their aspirations by Leverhulme's plans, the land-hungry men who had their sights set on the farms of Coll and Gress were beginning to vent their frustration even before 1918 was out.

On December 11th, a group of them wrote to the Board of Agriculture: "We as men who fought for the land urge you to cut out Gress farm as soon as possible, before spring, so that we can build our houses during the good weather. We have two claims on Gress farm. One, that it was scheduled out in 1913 by the Board and two, that this new Act gives power to the Board to cut out any land suitable for cultivation.

If the Board will not accept our grievances or cut out land before spring, we will take such legal action as is necessary because it is our land and taken from our forefathers by bad laws." (15) They also wrote to the Secretary of State for Scotland, threatening to "take the law into our own hands" (16) if there was not a rapid division into crofts.

The men elected four office-bearers to act on their behalf. Murdo Graham of 35 Coll was chairman, John MacDonald, 11 Back, was appointed secretary, Roderick Murray of 9 Back became treasurer, while Malcolm Martin of 59 Back was made their president. A General Election was fought on December 14th 1918 and, for the first time, the Western Isles was a constituency in its own right. The land question was very much to the fore, with all three candidates proclaiming support for the division of the farmlands into crofts. Dr. Donald Murray, formerly Medical Officer of Health for Lewis and an anti-coalition Liberal, won the seat. He strongly believed that all the land capable of cultivation should be taken into crofting use, and he fought the election on the land issue. At the beginning of his campaign in October 1918 he said: "Those who have so nobly and bravely defended our country as well as as the dependents of those who made the supreme sacrifice have the first claim to the land." All of the candidates acknowledged the positive possibilities inherent in Leverhulme's acquisition of the island, and assumed crofting and industry to be perfectly compatible. They all believed, however, that the resolution of the land question left over from before the war was the first priority.

Lewis awoke on New Year's Day, 1919, to learn of the unspeakable tragedy of the *Iolaire* disaster. Amidst the general atmosphere of grief, despair and poverty, work started on Leverhulme's schemes during the weeks which followed. In a stunned island, they provided the focal point for a rare shaft of hope and optimism, that this could be the economic turning point. Mac Fisheries, conceived of as the vehicle for marketing the fish landed and canned at Stornoway, was incorporated in February 1919. Up to this point, there had been no public indication of Leverhulme's determination to create a show-down round the future of Coll and Gress farms, which he had decided must not be broken up and should be used as dairy farms to supply the new industrial population of Stornoway with milk. If the men who warned of raids had known the half of what was going on behind the scenes, then it is doubtful if action would have been so long delayed.

As early as August 1918, alarm bells were set ringing in the Scottish Office when Thomas Wilson, the Board of Agriculture's representative on Lewis, met with Lord Leverhulme. Wilson was in no doubt about Leverhulme's genuine concern for the islanders, his energy or his willingness to invest a considerable fortune on his employment schemes, but was alarmed by the new proprietor's hostility to crofting. Lord Leverhulme told Wilson that crofting was "the worst possible form of tenure ... the constitution of additional small-holdings would only extend and aggravate a system thoroughly bad." (17) Wilson told his superiors: "I found it necessary very firmly to inform his Lordship that the condition he found the Lewis crofters in was very largely the result of the neglect of the former proprietors of Lewis." (18) Wilson doubted Leverhulme's understanding of the Lewis economy and its people. "His whole life has been industrial and I question if his experience of three months among the Lewis people has taught him their sentiments and desires. He does not realise that they will never feel satisfied until the farms in Lewis are divided and given to them." (19)

Thomas Wilson and his colleagues at the Board of Agriculture thus realised, within a few months of Leverhulme acquiring Lewis, that the schemes to create further crofts were in jeopardy. In October 1918, Leverhulme's representatives formalised this position by asking the Board of Agriculture that the Lewis resettlement schemes be put "on hold" for several years. "His Lordship is strongly of the view that the scheme put forward by the Board is not in the best interest of the islanders." (20) For the time being, the rigidity of Leverhulme's position remained private. Both the authorities and those who aspired to croft holdings knew that, for the first time in history, the law was on their side and that it was within the power of government to act. The Smallholders Act passed in 1911 extended the terms of the original 1886 Act, and formed the basis of future crofting legislation. Crucially it made provision for the landless squatters whose rights had been ignored in the original legislation. The Land Court and the Board of Agriculture replaced the Crofters Commission and the Congested Districts Board. The Board of Agriculture was also given the money to support its increased powers to take land into crofting use. These provisions had been strengthened by legislation passed in 1916 and 1918, while the Bill which was to become the Land Settlement (Scotland) Act 1919, greatly increasing the funds available to the Board of Agriculture and extending their powers to compulsorily acquire land, was making its way through the House of Commons. (21)

Politically it was a propitious time for the crofters. The promise of a land fit for heroes gave a new imperative to the land question in general. There was apparently support from the Government, and particularly from Robert Munro, Secretary for Scotland. Munro was a Highlander and the son of a Free Church minister from Easter Ross. Apart from being very much on the side of the crofters personally, Munro knew the dangers of reneging on any of the promises made before the war. In 1917, before Lord Leverhulme entered the picture at all, both Robert Munro and T.B. Morrison, the Lord Advocate, had spoken publicly in favour of the crofters' demands. Shortly before the outbreak of hostilities Munro had been seriously considering a proposal from the Lewis Crofters Association that the Government should purchase Lewis on behalf of its inhabitants. He knew the Lewis background and the potential for trouble.

Lord Leverhulme was perfectly aware of the strength of feeling and the determination, in all quarters, to redistribute the land which remained in the hands of tenant farmers. He was also familiar with all of the land settlement legislation and recognised the certainty of confrontation if he stood in the way of the ex-servicemen's aspirations. Nonetheless, that was the path which he had chosen to go down. In a letter to Sir Robert Greig, Chairman of the Board of Agriculture, he vowed to "oppose to my last breath and last penny all the attempts to perpetuate the present degrading conditions of the crofter's home and life that is rapidly bringing consumption and enfeeblement on one of the finest races of people the world today possesses." (22) In a fine balancing act, the Board sought to encourage Leverhulme's development plans while at the same time rejecting his proposals for the farms. In the early correspondence with the new proprietor the Board's strategy was conciliatory; they could see no great conflict between industrial production and agriculture. "Both can be carried out concurrently with mutual advantage...The people of Lewis, accustomed to crofting tenure, would not readily accept any other but would, on the contrary, be likely to press for completion of the Board's proposals whatever other steps might be taken to ameliorate existing conditions." (23) But by early March 1919, the time for conciliation had run out. Leverhulme's true intentions as far as the farms were concerned could no longer be avoided.

The nearby Tong Farm, three miles north of Stornoway, was the first to be raided. Like Coll farm, Tong was too small to have been scheduled by the Board of Agriculture. The raiders marked out lots covering 30 acres. On March 8th, Gress farm was raided. Forty men drove off Liddle's stock and replaced it with their own; they then began to turn the land and plant potatoes. (24) Similar action followed at Coll.

The police report of the raids said: "It would appear there is a solid determination to use the land and retain it for their own use. At Coll the villagers of Back and Coll started cultivating the field to the rear of the farmhouse. Soon lots were being pegged out throughout the farm. Men tilled the soil while women carried creels of seaweed from the shore to fertilise the land. On the following day the crofters' stock was placed on the farm grazings. Neither Charles Hunter, the Coll farm tenant, or Peter Liddle received threats of any kind." (25)

On March 11th, Leverhulme decided to meet the raiders on their own territory and called a meeting at Back schoolhouse. He described to the meeting his vision for Lewis, and asked them to consider the future. On that very day, he told the crowd, the contracting firm Robert MacAlpine had landed materials for the construction of the first 300 new houses for Stornoway. These would accommodate the industrial workers brought in from the country areas. Leverhulme appealed for his schemes to be given a chance. "All my life I have worked with people, not against them. I am not working against you... I ask you to give my schemes a ten-year trial. Surely that is not unreasonable for a problem that is one hundred years old." (26)

The following day, he arranged to meet with the Gress raiders. Over a thousand men and women gathered at Gress bridge "a sullen crowd resentful of the situation which had developed," wrote Colin MacDonald, a Board of Agriculture officer who had been sent to Lewis to negotiate with the landlord and had accompanied him to Gress bridge. Leverhulme stood on an upturned barrel in the centre of the crowd and, with carefully chosen words, began to address the crowd. "So great is my regard for Lewis and its people that I am prepared to adventure a big sum of money for the development of its resources and its fisheries." He told them of his plans to spend over £5 million on a great fishing fleet, a large fish canning factory, railways, an electric power station... Stornoway would become a beautiful garden city. There would be steady work and steady pay ... another great fleet of cargo boats, and so on.

It took a very brave man to intervene but Leverhulme was dealing with people as articulate as himself. One of the ring-leaders, Alan Martin, interrupted Leverhulme's fine flow and in an impassioned voice addressed the crowd in Gaelic: "Seo seo, fhearaibh! Cha dèan seo an gnothach! Bheir am bodach mil bheulach tha 'n sin chreidsinn ort gu bheil dubh geal 's geal dubh! Ciod e dhuinn na bruadair aige, a thig no nach tig? 'S e am fearann tha sinn ag iarraidh. Agus 's e tha mise a' faighneachd an toir thu dhuinn am fearann?"

Leverhulme's interpreter translated: "Come, come, men! This will not do! This honey-mouthed man would have us believe that black is white and white is black. We are not concerned with his fancy dreams that may or may not come true! What we want is land, and the question I put to him now is will you give us the land?" He answered emphatically: "No, I will not give you the land; not because I am vindictively opposed to your views and aspirations, but because I believe if my views are listened to if my schemes are given a chance the result will be enhanced prosperity and greater happiness for Lewis and its people."

Again he was interrupted, on this occasion in English by another of the raiders, John MacLeod: "I would impress on you that we are not opposed to your schemes of work; we only oppose you when you say you cannot give us the land, and on that point we will oppose you with all our strength. You have bought this island. But you have not bought us, and we refuse to be the bond slaves of any man. We want to live our own lives in our own way, poor in material things it may be, but at least it will be clear of the fear of the factory bell; it will be free and independent." (27)

There was to be no compromise on either side. Leverhulme was convinced he could bring the people round to his way of thinking, and while the crowd at Gress bridge may have been impressed with his fantastic vision, their cry for the land remained unaltered. Even if Leverhulme's ideas came to fruition, and there was strong scepticism on that score, the landless in Gress and Coll, and elsewhere on the island knew they needed crofts with security of tenure. They needed a secure base from which to work on the land and at sea.

The raiders left the farm in the autumn of 1919, to allow negotiations to be conducted in a less confrontational atmosphere. In the event, there was some conciliatory movement from Leverhulme. He started work on constructing a road from Tolsta to Ness and set aside part of the farms closest to Stornoway for quarter-acre lots for ex-servicemen, suggesting that if they wanted more land they could reclaim it from peat. "So this is your choice," he told the people of Back. "Either a quarter-acre allotment on part of the farms near Stornoway, or land reclaimed from the peat. Two thousand men can get quarter-acre allotments on 500 acres, but the ten-acre crofts, which some of you are demanding would take 20,000 acres, which is clearly impossible." (28) Nobody took up his offer.

There were to be no concessions in respect of the farms at Coll and Gress. These, he continued to insist, were to be used for the large-scale production of milk to meet the huge demand which he envisaged from the burgeoning industrial population of the town. Nigel Nicolson, the author of the most comprehensive book on Lord Leverhulme, claims that the question of milk production and supply on the island was a "bogey," but Leverhulme allowed the milk question to dominate all his thinking on farm policy.

In fact there was no shortage of milk in the town. Fifty gallons a day were imported from Aberdeen, and in the country every croft had a cow. Furthermore the imported milk was sterilised and refrigerated, and arrived in a better condition than much of the milk produced on the island. Nicolson comments: "The almost hysterical tones in which Leverhulme conducted this part of the argument ("will you let the children of this town die, or grow up as weak saplings?") suggests an untypical lapse in his sense of proportion.

"The farms were important, but not so important that their retention against the Government's policy was worth the sacrifice of all else. He dwelled on the milk supply as if it were a matter of great principle, when it was nothing more than a matter for administration and compromise." (29)

Thomas Wilson, from the Board of Agriculture, inspected the farms at Holm, Melbost, Stoneyfield and Manor, and advised the Board : "I have not the least doubt that from those farms an adequate supply of milk, for the present, could be got." (30) Leverhulme remained adamant. Gress and Coll were the prizes he was after, and he used the weekly £2,000 wage bill from his various enterprises as the stick with which to beat the raiders and the Board.

There is little evidence that, at this stage of his proprietorship, Leverhulme had the support of the majority of the people for his stance against the raiders. Thomas Wilson, in a general note to T.F. MacLean at the Board of Agriculture, wrote: "I have seen quite a lot of Stornoway people, and whatever they may say publicly, at heart they are all of the opinion the people should get the land, and they tell me so." (31)

The *Scotsman* similarly reported: "The attitude of the man in the street is also a trifle lukewarm. The sympathies of the Free Church are undoubtedly with the crofters.

Lord Leverhulme and party on the steps of Amhuinnsuidhe Castle.

In the disaffected regions the influence of the minister is being exerted to restrain them in the eyes of the law; but one Free Churchman told me he did not feel constrained to warn his flock against the seizing of the land." (32)

For many Lewismen, in a period of intense economic hardship, there was a great attraction in Leverhulme's apparent offer of economic prosperity. To most, however, there was no conflict between that sentiment and sympathy for the stance of the raiders since it was only Leverhulme who insisted that his schemes depended upon access to these particular farms for dairying. Only the editorial columns of the *Stornoway Gazette* and a coterie of the town's powerful bourgeoisie gave Leverhulme unqualified support. Leverhulme courted these sections of the population, and his largesse benefited business. Leverhulme entertained lavishly at the Castle, in the summer of 1918 he held the first of many fetes; his coming was then described by the local newspaper as: "an inrush of fresh life to the island." A leading businessman told a meeting in the town: "I believe that in the person of Lord Leverhulme, humanly speaking, the redeemer of our island has come among us." By August 1919, upward of 3,000 people attended one of his fetes in the Castle Grounds and all of that had some effect in gaining support for his ambitions. At the very least it divided loyalties. (33)

The *Stornoway Gazette* devoted many column inches to Lord Leverhulme's plans and often carried articles by the island's proprietor. Leverhulme used the paper to inveigh against socialism, bolshevism and anarchism; he was later to accuse the land-raiders of being controlled by communists. The paper's editorial, from the outset, backed Lord Leverhulme one hundred per cent. In January 1919 the editorial denounced the sceptics: "No Lewis man worth his name and worthy of the adventuring spirit of the pioneers who have made history in so many lands has had other than visions of Lewis yet to be happy and prosperous." The following month Leverhulme was made Right Worshipful Master of Lodge Fortrose, the local Masonic lodge.

Dr. Murray was probably Lord Leverhulme's most outspoken critic apart from the ex-servicemen during the early part of 1919. At a large gathering in Stornoway in May the MP said he was not prepared to scrap the convictions of a lifetime or electoral promises for anything he had seen or heard since the general elections five months previously. He said: "Everyone is willing to give the land to those who want it, wherever land is available. The Government promised them land. The BOAS scheduled certain farms on Lewis for division into small-holdings, and all political candidates to help the people get the land ... are all these promises to be thrown into the wastepaper basket as mere scraps of paper? These promises must be redeemed.

"I am not unmindful of the great industrial schemes which are planned by Lord Leverhulme for Stornoway and Lewis. I am full of admiration for the marvellous energy, the vision and the courage which characterise these vast conceptions, these schemes should be of great national benefit to Stornoway and indirectly to the

Robert Munro was Scottish Secretary during the post-war years. He played the difficult role of arbitrator between Leverhulme and the crofters.

Dr. Murray was the Chief Medical Officer of Health before becoming MP for the Western Isles. He was firmly of the opinion that Leverhulme's industrial schemes could exist alongside crofting and forcibly argued for that outcome.

landward parts of the island. There was always a large floating population in Lewis ready to engage in industry in any part of the country. I would be the last person to discourage any man or woman to work under these schemes. But as far as I can see there is no necessary antagonism between the old civilisation and the new ... there is room for both." (34) That seems to have been the prevailing point of view; very few were opposed to the schemes and most believed the two, industry and crofting, could co-exist without difficulty.

The unacceptability of Leverhulme seeking to use his ownership of the island in order to force through schemes at the expense of allocating small-holdings was also reflected in Parliamentary debate, notably when the Scottish Estimates were being discussed in August 1919. The Liberal member for Montrose, J. L. Sturrock, complained: "At the very moment when we have emerged from the greatest War in history, in the interests of liberty, he (Leverhulme) is taking it upon himself to tell these people ... that their future lives are to be guided along the lines laid down, not by themselves, not in accordance with the traditions of their ancestors, but according to the dictates of a successful soap-boiler who has happened to buy that island." (35)

In another powerful speech, Dr. Donald Murray spoke first of the great need in the islands for roads and fishery piers. He also acknowledged Leverhulme's spending on roads. "I want to be fair to him," said Murray, as the preamble to his remarks about the "most important question for the Highlands generally," that of land and small-holdings.

Murray recalled that he had travelled throughout Lewis in the first weeks of the War "and it was hardly possible to find a man capable of bearing arms. They were all away at the War. The women were tilling the soil, cutting the peats and keeping the home fires burning." These people deserved consideration, he continued. "They bought their freedom at a great price, and I think that even if great commercial magnates think that some other scheme is better for them, a little self-determination after all is a good thing.

"We are not such simple people as we look. It is said that the people are unwilling to leave those parts and prefer to stick to their poverty and misery because they do not know any better. The great bulk of the population of these islands, male and female, has been for years going round the coast of Great Britain. They have visited Wick and Aberdeen and Yarmouth and have been to Ireland. They know what their life is and they have sufficient common sense to know what is best for them. I hope industrialisation as we find it today is not the last word in the expression of social life." There were, said Murray, 800 applications for smallholdings from Lewis before the Board of Agriculture, and most of these had been submitted to it seven or eight years previously. He concluded by asking the Board to give the land in question to the people, "if necessary by compulsion." (36)

Just before the end of 1919 the Coalition Government passed into law the Land Settlement (Scotland) Act, which greatly extended the powers of the Board of Agriculture. Over £2 million was granted to the Board, partly to advance loans to the new settlers and partly to compulsorily buy land for settlement.

Leverhulme's grand design was, at this stage proceeding steadily. But suggestions were beginning to emanate from his camp that if the people of Lewis persisted with their demands for land and if the Government insisted on dividing the farms, Lord Leverhulme would wash his hands of the schemes. He made this threat as early as October 1919 at a meeting in Back when he told the raiders: "If you say you will not work with me then I will stop all development work in Lewis, and I will concentrate on Harris." He also vowed that those who seized the land would never get a croft on Coll and Gress should the farms be compulsorily purchased by Government. Thus the battle lines were drawn; after a little over a year as proprietor Leverhulme was contemplating this all or nothing ultimatum to the Scottish Office and the people of Lewis. He demanded a ten-year moratorium on the land re-settlement schemes; Coll and Gress would remain intact as large farms; and if ex-servicemen continued to raid the land he would pull out of Lewis altogether. On that basis he had harnessed the uncritical support of business and community leaders. This was the position which Leverhulme would maintain throughout his brief but stormy connection with Lewis. To many others on the island and elsewhere it seemed unnecessarily petulant and confrontational, paying no respect to the claims and expectations of the ex-servicemen.

The Raiders, Lord Leverhulme and the Board, 1920

"We are demanding nothing, but the promise that was made to us when we was ploughing the green ocean, and when we was in the earth holes in Flanders up to our knees in mud."

> Letter to Robert Munro, Secretary of State for Scotland, from Angus Graham, 71 Coll, Isle of Lewis; March 3rd, 1920.

"It is said the company is prepared to give us ex-soldiers little plots of land on the Sassenach Feu-right system. As a lawyer you know what that means. We know too. The Crofters Acts are to be thrown out at the stroke of a millionaire's pen. The rich are to lay down the law to the poor, and Lewis is to be shut off from the rights secured by the best Acts of Parliament ever passed for the benefit of the Highlands."

> Letter to Robert Munro, Secretary of State for Scotland, from Murdo Graham and Donald Campbell on behalf of the Gress and Coll ex-servicemen; August 11th, 1920.

At the turn of the year, the ex-servicemen re-occupied the land at Gress and Coll while reaffirming their intention of staying by preparing the foundations for temporary housing and making the ground ready for work in the spring. (37) Murdo Graham, Alexander Graham, Roderick and John MacDonald loaded their carts with stones from the dykes surrounding the potato field, and began to build the houses late in January. The raiders worked on the buildings as the weather allowed and on March 19th, Donald MacLean moved into the first completed house. Two months earlier the raiders had prevented farm employees from cultivating the soil.

Six of the men unyoked the horses and took the reins off Frank Clarke, the farm manager, and led the horses back into the stables. The raiders continued to cart seaweed from the shore to fertilise the land while the estate complained that its employees "were intimidated by threats of violence should they carry on carting the seaweed or cultivating the soil." (38)

Leverhulme was reluctant, at first, to interdict the men. He was not going to law himself, he told a Stornoway meeting in February. "The police and magistrates have a duty devolving upon them to maintain the law." His position was not one of lacking sympathy towards the raiders, he declared, but in the same breath warned: "The methods they are taking would in the short space of five years leave them with a starving rural population, absolutely needing to be fed." (39)

Leverhulme then dropped his first bombshell — he was going to give up on the rural areas altogether. (40) Crofting, he believed, was an impediment to progress and while he could attempt to take the landward areas around Stornoway out of crofting tenure, he regarded the distant country areas totally outwith his control. Henceforth Leverhulme's schemes were going to be concentrated in Stornoway, its environs and Harris.

Stornoway was to be entirely remodelled. Leverhulme declared it was his "dearly cherished desire to make Stornoway the finest city in the West of Scotland." His plans involved demolition of a large number of existing properties. The estate exercised a right of pre-emption over town properties which were for sale, and purchased them in order to knock them down if their location interfered with the proposed model town. (41)

The second and even more controversial announcement that February evening was of Leverhulme's decision to dismiss men employed on any of his schemes in Stornoway or elsewhere from "districts where farms had been raided." Sixty men from Coll, Vatisker and Back were immediately laid off. Leverhulme said: "I cannot sympathise with the indifference of the population of Back to the illegal acts nor can I find employment for men of that district." (42)

The move was designed to foster resentment against the raiders within their own communities and, together with the steady flow of anti-raider propaganda, it had immediate effect. Unemployed men, bitter that they should have been singled out and thrown on the scrapheap joined the anti-raider coalition. Community leaders, teachers, ministers and church elders were now pressurised by a very effective propaganda machine to denounce the ex-servicemen. A public meeting at Back led by the Rev. R MacKenzie of the Free Church told the men that their actions were causing great misery for others.

Because of the total absence of balance in the reporting of this and other meetings it is not clear what the raiders' response was. After lengthy accounts of speeches hostile to the raiders' cause, the *Stornoway Gazette* merely appended the curt statement that they "tried to justify their actions." (43)

A petition pledging loyalty to Lord Leverhulme and his schemes and asking to put the law in motion against the raiders was organised by the pro-Leverhulme lobby and signed by 7,000 people. (44) Other accounts from less partisan sources suggest that opinion was more divided and that sections of the community continued to back the raiders. (45) *The Glasgow Herald* reported: "Some said they would go home to bring moral suasion on their law-breaking neighbours, while others said the only course open to them was to join the raiders."

Colonel Walter Lindsay, Leverhulme's representative on Lewis, visited Back early in March and gave the raiders an ultimatum, either to withdraw or else the estate would initiate legal proceedings against them. The raiders chose to continue with their action and a few days later, Messengers at Arms set out to serve 32 men with interim interdicts. When they arrived at the raiders' homes they were met by the women, who refused to accept the interdicts but agreed to accompany the Messengers at Arms to where the men were building temporary homes. (46) In the event, the raiders ignored the summonses and a warrant was issued for their arrest on April 1st. (47) They appointed Donald Shaw, the Edinburgh lawyer with long experience in work on behalf of the Land League, to undertake their defence.

Two weeks grace had been allowed before the interlocutor became effective and during that time the Board and representatives of Lord Leverhulme attempted to strike a deal with the raiders. But this intervention by BOAS officials failed to resolve the impasse. They could only offer holdings on the rough moorlands — the only land which would be made readily available by the estate. Such land, covered mostly by heather and rock, was virtually incapable of cultivation, said the raiders.

The men did make an important concession, however. *The Scotsman* reported that "...they would give favourable consideration to any reasonable offer of land, in any suitable situation, providing the offer is made under the rights of crofting tenure." By this stage in the dispute the raiders were more convinced than ever of Leverhulme's longer term plans to replace crofting tenure, as far as was possible, with the "feu-right" system, which he favoured.

Days before the arrests were due another petition was sent to the Secretary of State signed by 800 people from Back pledging their support to the raiders. The petition called on Government to "enforce the provisions of the Land Settlement Act and other Acts, having for their purpose the settlement of ex-servicemen and others on the soil. We ought to know what is good for the community and we have no hesitation in affirming that no industrial schemes in Stornoway or elsewhere can solve the situation on the island. The people must have land first and homes to live in." (48) The petition was dismissed and denounced in the bitterest terms by the *Stornoway Gazette*. (49)

The Board were unable to deliver anything until the end of July when the estate suggested that the raiders should consider a move to Uig, almost 50 miles distance in the south-west of the island to settle on the farms of Reef, Ardroil, Carnish and Timsgarry with which Leverhulme had finally agreed to part. The offer, such as it was, was immediately rejected. The raiders said they had no interest in these farms "because there are plenty ex-servicemen there, some of whom have already raided these farms and need the land as much as we do." (50)

The impending arrests attracted outside media attention. In contrast to the one-sided reports carried by the *Stornoway Gazette*, The *Glasgow Herald's* version of

DEMOBILISED MEN RAID LEWIS FARMS

1 - The group of men who raided Gress Farm. 2 - Gress Farm.
3 - Men marking out their claims to the land.

events suggested that people were very much divided. They sympathised with the raiders but were also afraid of the impact of mass unemployment, should Leverhulme pull out. On April 12th, *The Glasgow Herald* reported: "The lack of immediate interest in the Leverhulme schemes is probably due to the fact that today most of them are, practically speaking, as much 'up in the air' as they were a year ago." Those who opposed the raiders feared above all that the proposed schemes would be scuppered sooner rather than later. Still others, reported the paper, "entertained the suspicion that the land revolt is encouraged and supported from the outside." The man from *The Glasgow Herald* could find no evidence to support these claims, but a month earlier the *Stornoway Gazette* had alluded for the first time to radical external influences guiding the hand of the raiders: "The Lewismen who have taken so unreasonable an attitude in regard to their claim for land and houses are not so much to blame as some person or persons of influence either within the island or outside it," declared its editorial darkly. The ex-servicemen's eloquent letters were an object of the *Stornoway Gazette's* scepticism: "Phrasing is so choice and the points so skilfully presented; if the authors are in every case raiders we have reason indeed to be proud of our crofters as a class at least as far as their powers of literary expression are concerned." (51)

These innuendoes were fuelled by developments in national and international politics. In the early 1920s, British papers were full of reports on the "Horrors of Bolshevism" in Russia, Ireland was in turmoil over partition and in this country the Labour Party and radical class-based politics had broken down the old Tory-Liberal domination. All over the country working people were withdrawing their labour, the Red Clydesiders were dominating class politics in the Scottish Lowlands and there was more than a whiff of revolution in the air. When John MacLean, the leading Glasgow communist, made an excursion to Lewis and expressed support for the raiders, his visit was hailed by the anti-raider coalition as vindication of their claims. Decidedly hysterical banner headlines in the *Stornoway Gazette* proclaimed: "Bolshevist in Lewis." (52)

There was not a shred of evidence to suggest MacLean or any other urban activists were advising or influencing the raiders. Indeed, such political intrigue must have seemed light years away from events on the ground, for the crofting year was in full swing. At Coll farm "a score of people, men and women, were busily engaged in turning the soil a good light loam with spades." This was the scene that greeted *The Glasgow Herald* correspondent when he visited the farm. The report continued: "In age and physique they were a mixed group. Most of the men were in the dark blue jerseys of the fisher class. The old man of 70-80 was more fluent in Gaelic than in English, and left the speaking to a man of about 30 years. The latter was sturdy, strong-shouldered and intelligent. His attitude was a curious blend of suspicion and amiability. He explained what they were doing and said they meant to carry on."

REPRESENTING THE RAIDERS

Mr Donald Campbell (Coll), right and Mr Murdo Graham (Gress), arranging with Mr Donald Shaw, S.S.C., for the defence of interdicted ex-servicemen. The latter served with the Gordon Highlanders and was severely injured in the left foot. The former was on a minesweeper during the war.

House-building was in progress, some were ready for occupation. The newspaper reporter asked if the men would continue to occupy the land "even if it means prison" and the raider responded: "Yes, we are prepared for the consequences." (53)

Lord Leverhulme was in Madeira while these events were unfolding, the raiders busy on the farmlands, apparently unconcerned about the legal proceedings which had been instigated against them, and the Board of Agriculture desperately trying to find a solution. However, at the eleventh hour Lord Leverhulme astonished everybody concerned by issuing instructions to stop all proceedings against the raiders.

The reason for this was that the Secretary of State for Scotland, Robert Munro, was prepared to call his bluff. Leverhulme's decision not to continue with the interdict and the arrests which were about to flow from it was a result of discussions between a director of Leverhulme's company, the Lewis and Harris Welfare and Development Company, and Munro. The latter made clear he had the power to release the men should legal action lead to their imprisonment. The Scottish Secretary refused to guarantee not to use his powers. (54) It was a stance which infuriated Leverhulme and left him potentially isolated. He complained bitterly of Munro's refusal to support the raiders' removal, but did not risk the humiliation of pressing for the men's imprisonment only to see them released again on Munro's instructions. His response was petulant and designed to provoke further hostility against the raiders within Lewis. It was announced that there was to be an almost immediate cessation of works.

Leverhulme's action was viewed with great dismay in all quarters. A mass meeting in Stornoway sent an appeal to the Secretary of State to draw the attention of Government to the "present impasse, and serious situation which will invariably follow from the cessation of Lord Leverhulme's development schemes; and further that they strongly petition the Secretary for Scotland to adopt and give effect to such a land policy for this island as will ensure the carrying out of these schemes by Lord Leverhulme." (55) This was the first indication that a substantial body of opinion within Lewis was prepared to abandon hard-won crofting legislation in favour of the landlord's schemes. For many who found themselves unemployed, no price was apparently too high.

A deputation of unemployed workers was dispatched to meet with the raiders and pleaded with the ex-servicemen that "crofting was not a profitable pursuit; to recognise the wisdom of Lord Leverhulme's plans; pledged to take whatever steps necessary to prevent opposition which may hinder the schemes; and finally that they wanted work, not land." (56) The Provost of Stornoway, Roderick Smith, on behalf of civic and business leaders, asked the Government to "take steps to get the opinion of the people of the island as a whole" before "undertaking to force a land policy that would be the means of stopping Lord Leverhulme's beneficent schemes" and urged Lord Leverhulme to "stay his hand in the meantime, until the Secretary of

State responded." (57)

Leverhulme chose not to stay his hand. If anything his intransigence intensified and became more irrational. The major lay-offs continued and the first post-war tide of emigration set in. All construction, drainage and road-building came to a halt. Only twelve workers were retained to complete the Garry Bridge. He told the Scottish Secretary that the schemes would only resume if the raiders withdrew and he was given possession of the farms.

In Parliament Dr. Murray described cessation of the works as "a very great disaster" but added: "My own view all along has been that there is no reason why the development of small-holdings and the developments of Lord Leverhulme's works should clash in any way." (58) The ex-servicemen also protested and reiterated the view that the taking of Coll and Gress had no bearing on the schemes: "There are several estate farms nearer Stornoway which are under pasture and could be utilised for the supply of milk." (59) The ex-servicemen also complained about the "one-sided character" of the Stornoway meeting which produced the civic and business leaders' declaration. All those who took part, they claimed, were "interested parties." (60)

The raiders had no access to the press and as a consequence their case was seldom heard. In an attempt to redress the situation they began to release, to the press, communications between themselves and the proprietor. They told Leverhulme "as so much had already appeared in the newspapers by way of stating your point of view, it is only fair that both sides of the question should now be laid before the public." (61)

In June the raiders wrote to Leverhulme requesting a meeting and offering a fair rent for the farms should he consider parting with them. The extraordinary response from Lord Leverhulme did nothing to soothe the attitudes of the raiders. It does, however, provide a most revealing insight into the mind of Leverhulme and how the issue of the farms had grown completely out of proportion. He told the men that he had wanted to provide 2,000 people with a quarter acre feu but they had prevented that by illegally seizing the land. "Your first act should be to reinstate yourselves as honest men, vacate the land you have illegally entered upon, then ... I shall be pleased to meet you."

Leverhulme continued: "The policy you have selfishly adopted will force the other landless men to emigrate to Canada and elsewhere. You are condemning them to be exiles from their own native lands... Your actions can only result, in a year or so, in your crops being raided and the fruits of your industry being taken by midnight thieves. This is always the case. The act of theft which you have committed will encourage other acts of theft. Your crops will not be safe, and finally your wives and children and your own lives will not be safe. You will get neither happiness or comfort from the crops you have taken." (62)

Lord Leverhulme with Stornoway businessmen.

The raiders' reply did not miss its target: "In the course of your long tirade you make frequent appeals to us to observe law and order forgetting that our record as law-abiding citizens will compare not unfavourably with yours. To you law and order evidently means liberty to starve us and our wives and children, by witholding from us the land created not by yourself, but by a greater Lord for the use of His people.

"Had you been really anxious to place the landless men of Lewis who are desirous of obtaining holdings you could easily have done so. It is cowardly therefore to blame us for your own unwillingness in that matter. It is also futile to throw dust, as you are doing, into the eyes of the public by making us appear as being opposed to your schemes... Our actions cannot interfere in the slightest with any scheme you have in hand ... but your stubborn attitude stands very much in the way of all schemes for setting people on the land. It is as silly as it is heartless of you to dismiss innocent men from your employment because you suspect they are in sympathy with our demands."

The letter concluded: "How can you safely be entrusted with the administration of this island if you are to exercise your great power so arbitrarily?" (63) That is a question which a great many must have pondered; not least, perhaps, Robert Munro when he so crucially refrained from giving Leverhulme the backing he demanded.

When Munro was due to visit the island in October, the raiders again wrote to state their case: "We should prefer to remain poor, if independent, than to be placed at the mercy of any individual or company which throws men idle at a moment's notice. It is foolish of certain misinformed organs of landlordism to malign us and condemn us because we refuse to be over-ridden." (64)

The Lewis District Committee and Stornoway Town Council had been busily engaged in promoting the opposing point of view, and began to organise public meetings and petitions throughout the island in advance of Munro's visit. In the event, he was unable to travel to Lewis in October, but the Lord Advocate, T.B. Morrison, went in his place. He was accompanied by Sir Arthur Greig of the Board of Agriculture; Sir Arthur Rose, Land Settlement Commissioner for the Board; and Thomas Wilson who was the BOAS sub-commissioner for the North West. They met Donald Campbell at Coll and afterwards visited some of the raiders at their homes, and then went on to Gress. The main meeting was held in Back school. Before it commenced the raiders' representatives complained at their treatment by the press, particularly the *Stornoway Gazette,* and requested that the press should be excluded.

In a statement after the meeting Morrison said there was nothing essentially antagonistic between a policy of land settlement and industrial schemes on the island. He said the raiders would consider whether to withdraw to allow further negotiations to take place. In Stornoway, Provost Roderick Smith led a deputation to see the Lord Advocate and pleaded the anti-raider case with vigour, but with much less success than they must have expected. By tying in their support for Leverhulme with ill-concealed disregard for crofting, they alienated the visitors. The outcome of the meeting was reported in *The Glasgow Herald*, with Morrison saying: "I would be sorry to think as one of the deputation had said, that the crofters' time was done." He thought that the question of development on the island had been very much looked at from the deputation's own point of view; the view taken in the town of Stornoway. (65) Great stock was placed by the raiders on Morrison's comments, which appeared to be a stinging rebuff to the Stornoway lobby. The *Stornoway Gazette* complained testily that the Lord Advocate had failed to "grasp the root facts of the situation." However, Morrison remained unpersuaded that there could not be a reasonable solution if only Leverhulme would take a more reasonable line. He described the confrontation as being due to "misunderstandings, extreme views and extreme measures." (66)

On October 17th, as a result of the Lord Advocate's visit, the raiders left the farm for a second time. Donald Shaw advised them to vacate the farm "in order to enable the Government and the Board of Agriculture to deal with the whole question of land settlement, and to permit the re-instatement of the men dismissed in Stornoway." (67)

Immediately after the raiders' withdrawal from Coll and Gress, Murdo MacAulay, secretary of the ex-servicemen's association who had backed Leverhulme's schemes telegrammed the proprietor asking him to deny rumours current in the town that "works are not to be re-started." (68) Leverhulme responded that there was no truth in the rumours and promised work would re-start in March the following year.

Stornoway Town Council and the Lewis District Committee continued to collect signatures urging Munro to accede to Leverhulme's request for a 10-year moratorium on land re-settlement schemes. Councillors travelled throughout the island and ultimately obtained widespread support for a resolution to this effect. (69) This at last appeared to provide the evidence of whole-hearted support for Leverhulme within the island which civic and business leaders had claimed but never previously demonstrated. It was obtained with the help of intense pressure exercised by people of influence within each community, against the background of a growing belief that Leverhulme was on the verge of turning his back on the island. Identical resolutions were put to meetings throughout the island. They asserted that "this representative meeting" of whichever area "heartily appreciates the development schemes for Lewis, voluntarily offered by the Right Honourable Lord Leverhulme...We, the inhabitants of the above-named townships undertake for at least ten years not to take part in the illegal raiding of any farm lands in Lewis, so as to give His Lordship the necessary opportunity and support he requires to make his schemes a success." (70)

By January 1921, the Lord Advocate's scepticism appeared to have been sidelined and the Scottish Secretary, Robert Munro, had acceded to Lord Leverhulme's request for a ten-year moratorium on compulsory take-over of land for crofting. Munro wrote to Leverhulme: "From the numerous resolutions which have reached me from meetings held throughout the island, I think I am entitled to assume that your policy is endorsed by a large section of the community." No compulsory purchase of land would take place while Lord Leverhulme's schemes were in operation. Crucially and presciently, Munro added that if the schemes did not proceed, "the hands of the Government will of course be free." (71)

It seems likely that the wave of public sentiment in favour of giving Leverhulme a chance on his own terms was encouraged by the growing suspicion that his schemes were in deep trouble anyway. In Stornoway, even before the raiders withdrew in October, there had been rumours suggesting that the schemes would never restart. Leverhulme denied them, but acknowledged that work could not get under way again until the spring of 1921. Certainly Munro would have known of the financial difficulties closing in on Leverhulme and that therefore the concession of the ten year moratorium, to be suspended if the schemes failed to proceed, was less dramatic a change of position than it appeared.

The speed with which Leverhulme's financial weakness was exposed, and therefore the brevity of the raiders' truce, could scarcely have been foreseen, however, as 1921 dawned.

The Final Years

"We. frequently hear that Lewis will be revolutionised and made very wealthy if the landless people will only consent to be dictated to as to how they should live, and above all if they will only consent to renounce all the rights to the land which have been won during your lifetime and ours.

"... His Lordship appears to be greatly disappointed that the jingling of his money bags is not sweet music to everyone, but you can tell him that we do not all lay up our treasure on this earth."

Letter to Robert Munro, Secretary of State for Scotland,
from Donald Campbell and Murdo Graham on behalf
of the Coll and Gress ex-servicemen, August, 1920.

"I only wish I possessed the requisite eloquence and facility of expression to put before you my case for the abandonment of crofting in a more convincing way than my limited powers permit."

Lord Leverhulme to Robert Munro, the Secretary of
State for Scotland, May 18th, 1921.

It seemed that Lord Leverhulme had finally got what he wanted. The raiders had left the disputed farms and the Government had given way. Leverhulme had not been required, in the end, to compromise as far as Coll and Gress were concerned though he had ceded the break-up of the Uig and west coast farms. A year earlier when Colin MacDonald from the Board of Agriculture advised him to reach a compromise with the raiders, Leverhulme responded: "I will not compromise. I must control ... I must have control of my factory hands! How can I have that in the case of men who are in the independent position of crofters?" (72) That was really the crux of Leverhulme's concern, and why he had fought the battle so intensively. It was crofting in general which he despised. Now, in January 1921, he was in control of Coll and Gress after almost three long years of conflict. But it was too late.

For reasons far removed from his Lewis operations, Leverhulme was facing financial trouble. According to Nigel Nicolson it was indeed "the severest financial crisis of his career," resulting from the problems of the Niger company. (73) In January, he gave orders for the remaining work which was then in hand on Lewis to be closed down. All of the private works around the Castle and grounds stopped and the

Employees of the Leverhulme Company LAHWAD (Lewis And Harris Welfare And Development Company Ltd).

remaining work on the houses at Goathill was suspended. Gamekeepers, gardeners and foresters were all laid off. This turn in events caused disquiet even among Leverhulme's most ardent supporters. William Grant, editor of the *Stornoway Gazette*, told B.P. Wall, Leverhulme's chief engineer, that the dismissals would undo "the whole of the good work among the people of Lewis which your Lordship's friends and well-wishers have striven to do during these critical times. He (Grant) desired me to convey the opinion that practically every farm will be raided before the Spring sowings." Wall reported to Leverhulme that the faithful editor "wanted to know what had occurred to induce your Lordship to make these reductions, but I said I had no information." (74)

Leverhulme was in severe financial straits. A confidential note between the Treasury and the Board of Agriculture suggested that there was "some doubt here as to the financial stability both of the firm (Lever Brothers) and Lord Leverhulme himself." (75) In fact, both were facing the possibility of bankruptcy, until Barclays Bank bailed the company out with a substantial loan against the issue of debenture stock, nearly all of which was held by the Bank. Leverhulme was no longer his own man and he told the 1921 annual meeting of Lever Brothers: "Until our debentures are greatly reduced, your directors would not feel justified in entering upon any new undertakings requiring cash capital." (76)

By February 1921 there were over 3,500 people out of work in Lewis. The continued suspension of work and the failure to obtain credible assurances from Leverhulme heightened scepticism about the likelihood of his grand plans ever actually coming to fruition. As Grant recognised, this immediately "put raiding back on the agenda, in Coll and Gress." Leverhulme's triumph had been short-lived and Pyrrhic. Negotiations between the Board of Agriculture and the raiders were ongoing. In February their lawyer, Donald Shaw, wrote a private note to the Scottish Secretary: "I am personally anxious that the industrial schemes should go ahead and I am prepared to use any means within my power to bring about a friendly agreement. My clients and families are suffering, however, so severely from want of land and proper dwellings that it is useless to expect them to give up their claims to these lands unless we are in a position to make a reasonable alternative offer." (77) He believed that Coll was less important to Leverhulme than the farm of Gress, and suggested on that basis that the Board ask Leverhulme to give Coll over to the crofters. (78)

Thomas Wilson of the Board of Agriculture also devised a scheme to release the outrun sections of both farms for crofting, leaving the arable free for dairy purposes. But the threat of bankruptcy had still not mellowed Lord Leverhulme's intransigence. He refused to part with either farm, in whole or in part. "There is not sufficient land," he told the Scottish Secretary, adding: "Even if every farm were taken up and cut into crofts, it would only satisfy one tenth of the applicants." Leverhulme went on to wax eloquent on his favourite theme: "We have been told on the highest authority that 'where no vision is, the people perish.' Surely there can be a little wider vision than to condemn men and women to a miserable existence on a croft, or the alternative of forced exile." (79) Leverhulme signalled another area of controversy for the Scottish Secretary to deal with, insisting that the raiders should not under any circumstances get crofts. "If crofts were practicable and in the best interests of the island, then such crofts should be allocated on some system to the most deserving applicants, excluding entirely each and every one of the raiders." (80)

By March 1921 it became clear that the stalemate was going to persist, and that the raiders no longer saw any reason to hold back. They were in exactly the same position as they had been before the War, while Leverhulme's schemes were in increasingly obvious disarray.

Again, it was the ex-servicemen's turn to try to force the Secretary of State's hand: "Please do not allow our desperate plight to be camouflaged by reference to some minor industrial works at Stornoway. These works may or may not mature; the signs are that they will not, as they are liable to be closed down at the slightest excuse. In any event, we are not skilled factory workers and such work would not benefit us or our class. It is necessary we should have land and proper dwellings. The Acts of Parliament passed for providing us with holdings is our Magna Carta, and as long as they remain law we consider it your duty to give effect to them. Once more we call on you to do so." (81)

Leverhulme re-started his works on a greatly reduced scale in April 1921, employing 140 men, but he was under constant pressure from the bank and it is likely as Nigel Nicolson suggests that these men were taken on to abate public criticism. On May 3rd, the raiders re-occupied the land at Coll and six days later, Leverhulme ordered the complete closure of his development works.

In reporting these developments to his superiors at the Board of Agriculture, Thomas Wilson said of the raiders: "I cannot blame them if they, for want of a solution by lawful means, resort in their straits to unlawful means for assuredly were I situated as they are, I would not hesitate about breaking the law, but would do so and accept the punishment with pleasure, rather than go on to the end of my life in the wretched hovels they reside in." (82) These were strong words. Wilson was putting his position firmly on the side of the raiders. He had spent years amongst the crofters of the North West and had a clear understanding of the appalling living conditions of squatter families.

Before announcing his pull-out, Lord Leverhulme had written to the Scottish Secretary seeking a guarantee that if he took legal proceedings against the men which would result in their imprisonment, Munro would not use his prerogative to release them. Again Munro could not accede to this request, and Leverhulme immediately announced the closure of all his work in Lewis. "I profoundly regret, under these circumstances, I have no course open to me but to stop all development work." (83)

Murdo Graham, one of the Gress Raiders, taken in the 1960s.

No action was taken against the Coll and Gress raiders; both Orinsay in the district of Lochs and Galson farm in Ness had also been re-occupied.

In June, Leverhulme's representatives met with the Secretary of State, pressuring him to the point of blackmail to stop the raiding, otherwise Leverhulme would pull out altogether. It was a heavy burden to place on any man, and Munro did try to offer solutions. He put alternative plans to the proprietor and told him: "I am satisfied that many if not all the troubles in Lewis would vanish, if you see your way to adopt the suggestions which I make. It does seem a pity that the whole future of the island for years to come should be jeopardised and indeed wrecked on account of a difference in policy regarding two small farms." (84)

After his meeting with Leverhulme's representatives, the Scottish Secretary contacted Donald Shaw who in turn advised the raiders to withdraw and refrain from raiding because: "I am sceptical about Lord Leverhulme's intentions regarding the schemes and we should give him no excuse for abandoning works."

The Board of Agriculture held a similar view: "My opinion is that Leverhulme would be glad to get out of his industrial schemes and that he will use the Coll and Gress affair as his justification." (85) The same letter pointed out that there were more men employed on road-making in Lewis before the advent of Leverhulme than there had ever been since. The raiders completely withdrew from the farms for the third time but continued to press their case. Ten raiders went to Gress Lodge and asked for work. When they were refused, the deputation told the farm manager: "We have no land and no crops for the winter. We do not intend to starve while potatoes are growing on the land next to us."

This was interpreted by the estate as yet another threat to raid. And it was sufficient to precipitate the final closure of the little work which remained. Even when the raiders did not carry out their threat at Coll and Gress, Leverhulme used the raid at Orinsay in the district of Lochs as justification for an end to his Lewis works. It was absolutely clear at this stage that raiding or the slightest threat of it was being used by Leverhulme as an excuse for a withdrawal which was really caused by the company's wider financial crisis.

The proprietor returned to the island in August, raising some hope of a change of heart on his part, but for those people who had pinned their hopes of employment on Lord Leverhulme there was only more disappointment. Leverhulme announced his last, and by far the most bizarre plan for the island. In a speech which he delivered to the Stornoway Agricultural Show, he suggested that the people ought to keep goats and sell heather. The island children were instructed to bring sack-loads of heather to the new, but empty, canning factory where it was to be boxed and sent over to the MacFisheries shops throughout the country. Needless to say the plans came to nothing; the supplies of heather which completely filled the canning factory were later used for horse bedding. (86)

A portrait of Murdo Maclean, 'Mòchan', one of the raiders.

© *Illustration by Andrew McMorrine*
Collection of Donald Maclean

There was no resumption of Leverhulme's work schemes in Lewis. At the end of what proved to be his last visit he told a gathering at the Stornoway Highland Games: "Three years ago it was mutually accepted that our relations would be on a strictly business basis; that there would be no odious taint of philanthropy to lower ourselves in each other's esteem. No-one regrets more than myself that the canning factory, the fish products and the ice companies cannot be opened for work. But the conditions of supply and demand in these industries make it impossible to do so. The business could only make losses, heavy losses if operated at present. We must wait patiently for the world markets to be cleared of surplus stocks before the prices will adjust themselves to the cost of production." (87) Similarly none of the construction works could proceed.

So when Lord Leverhulme finally pulled out of Lewis it was for reasons of economy and market conditions. Lever Brothers had experienced the biggest financial crisis in the company's history and were accountable to the bank, the country was in the grip of a recession and while there may have been returns from the Lewis schemes in the longer term, there had been no significant return on the cash already invested in the island by Leverhulme.

The Secretary of State was not prepared to wait for the possibility of Leverhulme returning in response to an economic upturn, but saw this as his opportunity to enforce the provisions of the Land Settlement Acts. He wrote to Lord Leverhulme: "In the circumstances as they are now I feel that I would not be justified in refraining any longer from putting into operation a generous measure of land settlement." Munro believed that Lord Leverhulme's suspension of all projects on the island amounted to a unilateral breach of the bargain between the two men. The ten year moratorium on land had been broken and the Government was free to compulsorily take over the disputed farms. (88)

Leverhulme agreed, however reluctantly, to let the farms of Coll and Gress go, though he thought the Scottish Secretary had shown "indecent haste" in tearing up the January agreement. He remained diametrically opposed to the Government's plans for the island, adding: "My views on the evils of crofting are not in any way altered; on the contrary the present position of the people of Lewis and their difficulty in finding employment has confirmed me in my views. It would be contrary to my convictions if I voluntarily gave up for crofting purposes the farm lands for which you now apply, or consented to any partition of these farms." He would let the farms go, but only "subject to satisfactory terms being arranged." (89) The terms referred to by Leverhulme included the demand that none of the raiders should receive crofts; a stipulation which the Board of Agriculture sensibly ignored. Early in 1922 the Board of Agriculture took over the farms of Coll and Gress, as well as North Tolsta and Orinsay, creating 180 new crofts and 81 enlargements of existing holdings. In March, Leverhulme attempted to intervene in the allocation process, writing to Munro:

"I cannot consent to any crofts being allocated to raiders. I gave intimation of this in my speeches during the last three years. No raider's name can therefore be included amongst those to be balloted." (90)

The ballots at Coll and Gress were held on April 7th and 8th, by Thomas Wilson and Colin MacLean from the Board of Agriculture. Lord Leverhulme's chamberlain, Captain Fletcher, was present but did not raise the question of raiders being excluded until some days later, by which time all of the new crofts were already allocated. Eighteen Gress raiders and eight of the Coll raiders were given crofts.

"Many of those who had been balloted on the 7th and 8th of April, were actually cultivating their holdings when I was in Coll and Gress on the 13th. I was aware that the Lord Advocate had promised the raiders at Coll and Gress, that if they obeyed the law by withdrawing from those farms, that their illegal action would not militate against their applications for small holdings, and I am satisfied that Lord Leverhulme's representatives were also aware of that promise, and that an objection on the ground that an applicant had been a raider at Gress or Coll was inadmissible and would have been a breach of public faith. Of the 106 holders the majority were cultivating the ground, while all are arranging for removal to their future homes," wrote Thomas Wilson in November 1921. (91)

The persistence of the raiders had finally prevailed. If Lord Leverhulme had succeeded in his aim, not only would Coll and Gress have remained as farms but the whole principle of crofting tenure would have been called into question first in Lewis and then, inevitably, elsewhere. That was certainly Leverhulme's ambition. The raiders had faced up to the relentless weight of Establishment opinion, and the natural ambivalence of a population which desperately needed work. There were many extraneous factors which eventually determined the outcome of the conflict. But, fortunately for future generations, the test of will between the raiders and the arch enemy of crofting resulted in Coll and Gress being established as crofting communities.

Back Men who were allocated crofts at Gress:

No.	1	Murdo MacLeod (Murdo)
	2	Kenneth Ferguson (Goididh)
	3	Murdo Murray (Murchadh Uisdein)
	5	Murdo Graham (Murchadh Seònaid)
	7	Allan Martin (Allan Tharmoid)
	8	Alex John MacDonald (Spring)
	9	Alex Graham (Alaic Alasdair Bhig)
	10	Roderick MacLeod (Roddy Dhòmhnaill Duinn)
	11	Alex MacLeod (An Caolais)

12	Angus MacLeod (Aonghas Ceanaidh)
13	Murdo MacLeod (Murchadh Barrant)
14	William Munro (Tuliban)
15	Murdo MacIver (Sgaoisidh)
16	Neil MacLeod (Ughlag)
17	Evander Ferguson (Elib)
19	Evander Ferguson (Iomhair Teel)
20	Donald MacLeod (Dòmhnall Beel)
21	Angus MacLeod (Aonghas a' Bheel)
24	Kenneth Morrison (Coinneach Saor)
25	Donald MacLean (Crùbag)
26	John Murray (Iain Uisdein)
27	John MacDonald (Sgineach)
28	Roderick Murray (Cèic)
29	Hugh Stewart (Heech)
30	John MacLeod (Iain Dhòmhnaill)
31	Alex MacLeod (Boibsidh)
37	John MacLeod (Iain an t-Siaraich)
38	Murdo Graham (Beag)
39	Roderick MacDonald (Ruairidh Portar)
40	Murdo MacDonald (Prize)
41	Angus Graham (Sailor)
42	Angus MacLeod (Aonghas Cleòid)

Notes and References

1. SRO AF 83-354. Letter dated September 1918, detailing the meeting between Leverhulme and Thomas Wilson.
2. All the pre-war files are contained in SRO AF 83 360/362. See also Leah Leneman, *Fit for Heroes? Land Settlement in Scotland after World War 1*, Aberdeen, 1989, chapter 6, Schemes in the Long Island.
3. Ibid.
4. Ibid.
5. Ibid.
6. Ibid., *Fit For Heroes? Land Settlement in Scotland after World War 1*, Aberdeen, 1989, ch.7.
7. SRO AF83/360.
8. SRO AF83/354.
9. SRO AF83/360. In the summer of 1917 the Board were preparing the schemes in order to launch them immediately after the War.
10. SRO AF83/360. See also Leah Leneman, *Fit For Heroes? Land Settlement in Scotland after World War 1*, Aberdeen, 1989, p118.
11. SRO AF83/354.
12. Nigel Nicolson, *Lord of the Isles*, London, 1960; this is a good account of Leverhulme's time in Lewis and of his various activities in Africa. See also W.P. Jolly, *Lord Leverhulme: A Biography*, London, 1976.
13. Letter dated 26th Sept, 1918, from Lord Leverhulme to Thomas Wilson, the Board of Agriculture's senior sub-commissioner for the area.
14. *Stornoway Gazette,* throughout the period. The first garden party was held in July 1918.
15. SRO AF67/147.
16. SRO AF83/363.
17. SRO AF83/354 account of Wilson's first meeting with Leverhulme; his report to the Chairman of the Board of Agriculture is dated Sept. 26th, 1918.
18. Ibid.
19. Ibid.
20. SRO AF83/354 letter dated October, 1918.

21. Leah Leneman, *Fit For Heroes? Land Settlement in Scotland after World War 1*, Aberdeen, 1989. The first chapter looks at the various pieces of legislation.
22. SRO AF/83 letter from Lord Leverhulme to the BOAS dated October, 1918.
23. Ibid., letter from the Secretary of State to Leverhulme, August, 1918.
24. SRO AF 67/324 Police Report of the raid.
25. Ibid.
26. *Stornoway Gazette*, March, 1919.
27. Colin MacDonald, *Highland Journey*, Edinburgh, 1943.
28. *Stornoway Gazette,* August, 1919.
29. Nigel Nicolson, *Lord of the Isles*, London, 1960, 132.
30. Telegram from Thomas Wilson to T.F. MacLean at the BOAS, dated 17th April, 1920.
31. Ibid.
32. *The Scotsman.*
33. *Stornoway Gazette*, August 26th, 1919.
34. *Stornoway Gazette*, May 9th, 1919.
35. *Hansard,* Scottish Estimates, August 4th, 1919.
36. Ibid., Nigel Nicolson, *Lord of the Isles*, London, 1960.
37. Threats of futher raids were reported as early as December 26th, 1919, in the *Stornoway Gazette.*
38. *The Glasgow Herald,* January 16th and 19th, 1920.
39. *The Glasgow Herald*, February 10th, 1920.
40. Ibid.
41. Nigel Nicolson, *Lord of the Isles*, London, 1960.
42. *Stornoway Gazette,* March 5th, 1920.
43. Ibid.
44. *Stornoway Gazette*, April 2nd, 1920.
45. *The Glasgow Herald*, February 10th, 1920. See also SRO AF67/255.
46. *The Glasgow Herald*, April 9th, 1920.

47. Interlocutor for the arrest of the men: SRO67/325.
48. Telegram to the Secretary of State dated April 3rd, 1920.
49. *The Glasgow Herald*, April 16th, 1920.
50. There were raids concurrently in Uig, Lochs and Ness.
51. *Stornoway Gazette*, March 19th, 1920.
52. Ibid., April 13th, 1920.
53. *The Glasgow Herald*, April 10th, 1920
54. SRO AF67/147, also quoted in Nigel Nicolson, *Lord of the Isles,* London,1960, in an extract from Leverhulme's farewell speech in Stornoway.
55. SRO AF/255.
56. *Stornoway Gazette*, May 28th, 1920.
57. *The Glasgow Herald*, May 10th, 1920.
58. *Hansard,* July 1st, 1920.
59. *The Glasgow Herald*, May 21st, 1920.
60. Ibid.
61. *The Glasgow Herald*, June 26th, 1920.
62. *The Glasgow Herald*, June 10th ,1920.
63. Ibid.
64. Letter to Robert Munro dated August 11th, 1920.
65. *The Glasgow Herald*, October 1st, 1920.
66. *Stornoway Gazette*, October 15th, 1920.
67. *The Glasgow Herald*, October 17th, 1920.
68. *Stornoway Gazette*, October 22nd, 1920.
69. SRO AF67/555 resolutions dated January 11th, 1921.
70. Ibid.
71. SRO AF67/389 Munro's letter aceeding to the 10 year delay in implementing land settlement.
72. Colin MacDonald, *Highland Journey,* Edinburgh, 1943.
73. Nigel Nicolson, *Lord of the Isles,* London, 1960.

74. Ibid.
75. Leah Leneman, *Fit For Heroes? Land Settlement in Scotland after World War 1*, Aberdeen, 1989, p121. Nigel Nicolson, *Lord of the Isles*, London, 1960, pp 165-7.
76. Nigel Nicolson, *Lord of the Isles,* London, 1960. W. P. Jolly, *Lord Leverhulme:a Biography*, London, 1976.
77. SRO AF67/331 private letter from Donald Shaw to Robert Munro.
78. SRO AF67/331.
79. Ibid., letter from Lord Leverhulme to Robert Munro dated May 18th, 1921.
80. Ibid.
81. Ibid., letter from Murdo Graham to Robert Munro dated March 3rd, 1921.
82. Ibid., letter to Robert Munro from Thomas Wilson dated May 4th, 1921.
83. Ibid., letter from Lord Leverhulme to Robert Munro dated May 9th, 1921.
84. Ibid.
85. SRO AF67 331 Letter from the BOAS to J. Lamb at the Scottish Office.
86. Nigel Nicolson, *Lord of the Isles*, London, 1960.
87. *Stornoway Gazette*, September 3rd, 1921.
88. SRO AF67 331 Letter dated September 3rd, and dispatched to Lord Leverhulme from Robert Munro on September 6th, 1921.
89. Ibid., correspondence relating to the allocation of crofts on the farms of Coll and Gress.
90. Ibid.
91. Ibid.

5 The Wider Struggle

"The Government has no more need for us at the present time. We were thrown into the furnace against the foe, and by the foe. What do we find now? A warrant granted to put us in prison.

"The Secretary of State for Scotland said that the fact of Lord Lever and Co. buying the island changes the circumstances. We beg to ask in what respect more than any other Landlord in Scotland? Both Lord Lever and the present Government wants to keep us in bondage —no freedom, no land, no homes. We beg to say once and for all: until this burning question is settled there will be no rest in the Highlands and Islands.

"We pray to God that something will come about soon that will give us freedom, land and a home for our families at a fair rent."

> John MacAulay, 3 Islivig, Uig, Isle of Lewis, and others, letter to Secretary of State, Robert Munro, dated April 10th, 1920. (SRO AF67/255)

"The raiders' action in declining to recant, when offered a free pardon if they promised not to go back to Reef again, has produced a profound sensation amongst the prisoners' friends who have been informed that the raiders would prefer to go on suffering for a season rather than go against their consciences and their principles."

> *The Scotsman*, March 26th, 1914, referring to the men imprisoned in Edinburgh for raiding the farm of Reef.

The preceding chapters have focused on the sequence of events which led to crofters in four districts of Lewis reasserting their claims to land which had traditionally been worked by their forebears, but had been lost through eviction and clearance in the course of the nineteenth century. Lands formerly used for grazing were taken over by the Lewis landlords and used first for big sheep farming and then from the 1850s as deer forests. Where there was good arable land the villages were systematically cleared and a farmer, paying a greater rental, put in their place. The same process was experience in other parts of the island and this account would be incomplete without brief reference to the struggle for land elsewhere in Lewis.

For instance, the West Side of the Island between Shawbost and Carloway was the scene of bitter exchanges during the 1880s as a result of an injustice which had festered since the 1850s. At that time, the villages of Dalmore and Dalbeg were cleared. Unusually in rural Lewis, Dalbeg had an inn. The lands of the two villages, as well as the best part of the South Shawbost grazings, was given to the innkeeper to form a single farm. Families who had been removed from Dalmore and Dalbeg increased the overcrowding in Carloway and Shawbost. In the fevered climate of 1884, this was a natural location for raiding and the demand for redress. The walls which the crofters had been forced to build, to separate their own grazings from the extended Dalbeg Farm, became the targets for "dyke-breaking" on an extensive scale. Some of the other tactics used against authority were unusually militant, including what *The Scotsman* described as a "dastardly outrage" when boulders were placed across the road at Carloway in an apparent attempt to wreck a carriage conveying two officials of the Matheson Estate. (1) Several court cases ensued, as the crofters repreatedly drove their cattle onto the contested land. In 1887, their efforts were partially rewarded, when parts of the Dalmore and Dalbeg grazings were restored to crofting use after a lapse of more the 30 years, on the authority of the newly-appointed Crofters Commission.

Galson Farm, in the Ness district, was also target for raiding in 1887-88, inspired by the Park Deer Raid and at the same time as events were unfolding at Aignish. On December 21st 1887, 300 landless men from Borve and Shader marched on the tenant of Galson, a Mr. Helm, and warned him to leave when his lease was up. The marines who arrived on the Island to deal with the Aignish disturbances were also deployed around Galson, and representatives of the Borve and Shader men were present when Lady Matheson was petitioned in Sotrnoway on January 5th 1888 and delivered her classic rebuke: "These lands are my property and you have nothing to do with them." Galson was not eventually broken up until the end of the Leverhulme era.

The people of Uig in the South West of the Island arguably suffered more at the hands of the Landlords than anywhere else. It had more farms and deer forests, many hundreds were evicted and those who did not emigrate were crowded into the few remaining villages. By 1880 the population of the parish was 60 per cent greater than in 1,800 but it was crowded into little more than half the area of land. The extensive hill and mountain grazings, most of the best wintering ground and all the machairs except Valtos and Kneep were taken out of crofting use. (2) When the Napier Commission met at Miavaig in 1883, Norman Morrison from Breanish, at the southern tip of Uig, illustrated the effect of this contraction of land: "once you pass Valtos there is not a crofter between that and my own house — a stretch of ten miles. These ten miles are in the hands of two individuals, and on the other side of our village there is a twelve mile stretch till you reach Harris and there is no-one there except big sheep and shepherds." (3) At the other end of the parish 70 families were crowded into Valtos and Kneep. The greater part of their grazings, including the small offshore islands where they had summered the cattle, had gone to Reef Farm.

These were the circumstances which drove the Uig people to raid the farms first in 1884 and then intermittently until the 1920s. Towards the end of 1884, *HMS Assistance* with a force of up to 100 marines on board arrived in Loch Miavaig to effect the arrests of eight Valtos men accused of placing their stock on the off-shore islands for grazing, not paying their rents and deforcing Sherriff's Officers. The men were sent for trial to Edinburgh and served time in prison. (4) The following year a further ten men and seven women were arrested for related but separate incidents. Not a year went by without pleas being sent to the Scottish Office by the Uig crofters desperate for land and their demands intensified in the first decade of this century.

On Christmas Day 1908, 46 crofters and squatters met at the schoolhouse in Breanish and passed eight resolutions demanding the breakup of Mangersta and Carnish farms: "So that without leaving the locality where they were born and where all associations and kinshiops that make life dear are, the squatters hold that more than enough suitable land can be had." Failure to accede to these demands would result in the squatters taking "forcible possession and standing by the consequences." The petition was sent to Major Matheson, MPs — including the socialist Victor Grayson, who sat for distant Colne Valley — the Scottish Secretary and the press. (5) It contributed to securing at least part of the desired effect. Two years later Mangersta farm was broken up and thirteen new holdings created.

In Reef, raiding continued until war broke out in 1914. In the closing months of the previous year, the farm was raided on three occasions by squatters from Valtos and Kneep, who drove the stock of Alexander MacRae, the farmer, to Timsgarry where his father was tenant. In January 1914, the raiders began to turn the ground at Reef and mark out crofts. Interdicts were taken out by the Matheson estate and MacRae, against 18 men. When the interdict was broken on February 10th, the raiders were cited to appear in the court of session in Edinburgh on March 19th. (6) They arrived penniless in Stornoway and a subscription of £15 was raised before they could leave for the capital.

In the Court of Session, they were each jailed for six weeks. This gave rise to much indignation throughout Scotland, and a campaign to secure their release led to them leaving prison and returning home to a heroe's welcome after two weeks. Such were the events which were going on in Lewis, right up to the outbreak of the First World War when all such matters, as far as Parliament and the Scottish Office were concerned, went into abeyance. Many of those who had been desperate for land went off to fight, but it is reasonable to assume that never a day went by without thought of the unfinished business in their own communities. For those who survived, the contrast between their country's call to arms in this terrible war and its continuing failure to make good promises of land was incomprehensible and impossible to accept.

In Uig as elsewhere, raiding was on the agenda as soon as the War had been won.

With Leverhulme established as proprietor, landless men proceeded to cut peats and plant crops in Carnish. In a letter to the Board of Agriculture in March 1920, Malcolm Morrison from Islivig intimated that they had taken possession of Carnish "and tomorrow we intend to start building temporary houses here." (7) Like their compatriots in Coll and Gress, the Uig crofters continued to press their case with the Scottish Secretary. It was still a long haul, but, in Uig, Leverhulme agreed reluctantly to concede — perhaps as a pawn in his wider dealings with the Secretary of State for Scotland over the farms closer to Stornoway — to break up the farms of Carnish and Reef, as well as Valtos and Timsgarry, in 1921.

All crofting communities continued to face immense economic difficulties in the years and decades which followed. Emigration continued on a large scale throughout the 1920s, until world-wide recession set in. But gradually, conditions in rural Lewis improved. Modern houses were built. Government agencies were pressurised into developing forms of support.

When these better times came, the fact that a substantial crofting population still existed to take advantage of them was due in large measure to the courage and determination of previous generations who had challenged authority and asserted the people's claim to the land — Na Gaisgich.

Notes and References.

1. I.M.M. MacPhail, *The Crofters' War*, Stornoway, 1989.

2. *Royal Commission on the Highlands and Islands, 1883, (Napier Commission)*. See the evidence of Murdo MacLean, Valtos, 13672-13783.

3. Ibid., see the evidence of Norman Morrison, Breanish, 13848-13925.

4. I.M.M. MacPhail, *The Crofters' War*, Stornoway, 1989.

5. SRO AF59.

6. SRO AF67/61. Police Reports from P.C. Kenneth MacIver, Miavaig, containing details of raids in 1913-14.

7. SRO 67/62/65.

6 Selected songs and poems

Oran air Bill nan Croitearan

'S gun deachaidh an crann chur air an fharadh,
    'S talamh an arain a chur fàs;
Siud an rud tha uainn air aiseag
    Bh' aig ar n-athraichean air mhàl;
'S nam faigheamaid a-rìs air ais e,
    Cha bhiodh ar gearan ris an stàit
Airson gach cunnart agus mearachd
    Rinn fir an fhearainn air na Gàidheil.

Cuiridh sinn air falbh gach geamair,
    'S gach fiadh tha 'g ithe fearann àir,
Gan ruagadh suas a-rìs dhan fhireach,
    Agus thig na *Nimrods* bhàn;
Thèid na Sasannaich a thilleadh
    O bhith tighinn idir chun an àit',
Bhon rinn iad gu tur ar milleadh
    Le fèidh na beinne bhith cur fàs.

Is gun robh a' chaora fhèin co-ionnan
    Ga ar sgioladh chun a' chnàimh;
Chuir i 'n imrich air na h-iomadh
    Sìos gan iomain chun na tràigh;
'S iomadh uair a phian e m' innibh
    A bhith cho minig na mo thràill,
Is caor' is fiadh bhith air an innis
    A bheireadh biadh dha iomadh Gàidheal.

Ach thèid an crann a thoirt dhen fharadh
    'S thèid na gearrain chur an sàs,
Is treabhar sìos leo talamh an arain,
    'S gheibh na h-ainnisich an sàth;
'S gum bi crodh air sliabh gu bainne
    Anns gach baile mar bu ghnàth,
'S cha tèid sinn sìos gu iasgach Ghallaibh,
    Gheibh sinn aig a' bhaile màl.

'S cha bhi (sinn) strìochdte don a' Bhile
    Thug an *government* an àird;
Chan eil stiall ann airson criomaig
    Anns an cuireadh duine bàrr;
'S e tha sinne 'g iarraidh ionad
    Sam biodh ionaltradh nam bà,
'S an talamh ìosal airson mine
    Don a' ghinealach tha fàs.

Song about the Crofters' Bill

The plough has indeed been placed on the cross-beam,
and the arable land has been laid waste;
what has been taken from us is nothing less than
what our forefathers had on rent;
and if we were able to recover it,
we would not make our complaint to the state
concerning every danger and injustice
that the landowners have inflicted on the Gaels.

We will drive away every gamekeeper,
and every deer that consumes arable land,
chasing them up again to the deer-forest,
and the *Nimrods* will be brought low;
the English will be repulsed
from coming near the place at all,
since they ruined us completely
by laying waste (our land) with the deer of the hill.

The sheep itself was just as bad
in nibbling us down to the bone;
it caused many to migrate,
driving them down to the shore;
many a time it pained my guts
to be so frequently a slave,
while sheep and deer were on the pasture
that would have fed many Gaels.

We will not submit to the Bill
that the government has introduced;
it contains nothing with regard to a patch
where a man could plant a crop;
what we want is a place
where cows could find grazing
and the low land to produce meal
for the growing generation.

But the plough will (again) be taken off the cross-beam,
and the garrons set in harness;
the arable land will be ploughed by them,
and the poor folk will get their fill;
and the cows will be on the hill to produce milk
in every township as was customary,
and we will not go down to the Caithness fishing -
we will get rent-money at home.

Note:
This poem was composed by John MacRae, Lochcarron, and recited by him in Lochcarron Schoolhouse on March 11th, 1886. It was published in OT, March 20th, 1886.

Croitearan Leòdhais

'S e 'n t-iongantas as mìorbhailich
Bha riamh an Eilean Leòdhais,
Na daoine bochda riaghladh ann,
'S na tighearnan gan cur fòdhp';
Tha iad an-diugh le fialachd
A' tighinn a dh'iarraidh bhòts,
'S chan fhaigh iad uainn am bliadhna iad
Ge brèagha an cuid sgeòil.

A Chlann nan Gàidheal, còmhnaibh mi,
'S gun tòisich sinn a' roinn,
'S gun can sinn ris na h-uachdarain
Iad a dh'fhuireach uainn a-chaoidh;
'S gun seas sinn mar bu dual dhuinn
Le ar guaillean dlùth ri chèil',
'S gun toir sinn uile buaidh orr'
Le fear na gruaige lèith.

Nach b' e 'n Dotair Dòmhnallach
An t-òlach air an ceann;
'S ann dha as aithn' na dòighean
San toir e chòir gu ceann;
'S tha mise cur mo dhòchais
An slògh an eilein duinn,
Gun toir iad dha gach bhòt
'S gun seas e chòir don cloinn.

Ach fhuair e nis gach bhòt
'S tha dòchas agam fhèin
Gun seas e nis a' chòir dhuinn
An aghaidh fòirneirt ghèir;
'S tha mise guidhe tròcair
Ma dheònaiches tu fhèin
Nach till thu ris an t-seòrsa
Tha an còmhnaidh ris a' bhrèig.

An-diugh gur mis' tha uasal
As an t-sluagh dom buin mi fhèin,
Gach fine 's treubh 's na bhuaineadh —
Cha d' fhuaireadh iad toirt gèill;
Is ged tha daoine suarach
A' cosnadh duais dhaibh fhèin,
Tha Siorrachd Rois a' buadhach,
'S na h-uachdarain cha ghèill.

Bu tàmailteach le uaislean
Nuair chualas leo an sgeul,
Na daoine bochd' a' buadhach
Bha suarach aca fhèin;
'S gun choisinn siud do uachdarain
Bha uasal asda fhèin
Bhith gealltainn dhuinne duaise,
Nan cuirte suas iad fhèin.

Ged tha sinn bochd, gun d' fhuaireas
Sinn uasal seach iad fhèin;
Is thugadh iad an duaisean
Don t-sluagh a tha leo fhèin;
Cha chog sinn airson duaise,
Ach bheir sinn buaidh gu treun,
Is ceartas 's e ar suaicheantas,
'S cha ghabh sinn duais na brèig.

Tha breitheanas ro-uabhasach
Na thuarasdal don bhrèig;
Thug Iùdas fhèin a mhallachd oirr'
Ge b' eagallach a ghnè;
'S an duine reic am fearann,
  Bha peanas às a dhèidh;
Thuit e mar mar shamhladh,
'S a leannan às a dhèidh.

Nach b'e siud an t-uasal,
A lean an sluagh 's gach ceum,
Greenfield an duine uasal —
Cha mhealladh duaisean e;
'S fìrean tha ro-shuairce e,
'S do uaislean cha do ghèill,
'S cha ghabhadh e aon duais uap',
'S e 'g amharc suas gu nèamh.

Is aithne dhuibh *Novar* sin,
'S tha ghnùis ro-àlainn òg,
'S chan fhaicear e sa Phàrlamaid
Airson an àit' s' ri bheò;
Chan eil sinn airson uachdarain
Bhith riaghladh annns a' chùirt,
'S cha chreid sinn an cuid bhriathran
Gus am faic sinn gnìomh air tùs.

Tha oighreachd aig *Novar* sin,
'S chan fheàirrd e i san àm,
Na daoine bochd gan sàrachadh,
Gun àrach ac' don cloinn;
'S cha toir e sreath bhuntàta dhaibh
A bheir an tràth gu ceann —
'S e 'g iarraidh staigh don Phàrlamaid
Gu ar n-àite sheasamh ann!

The Lewis Crofters

The most amazing wonder
that has ever been in Lewis
is that the poor people are now ruling there
and the landlords trampled down:
today they are coming generously
to ask us for our votes,
but they will not get them this year,
however fine their tales.

Children of the Gaels, please help me
so that we can begin to discriminate,
and say to the landlords
that they stay away from us for ever;
And we will stand as we were accustomed
with our shoulders close together,
and we will all defeat them
by means of the grey-haired fellow.

Was not Doctor MacDonald
the hero at their head?
He is the one who knows the ways
of bringing justice to effect;
and I am putting my hope
in the people of this brown island,
that they will give him every vote,
and that he will stand their children's rights.

But now he has got all the votes,
and I myself have hope
that he will stand our rights for us
against oppression sharp;
and I pray that you'll get mercy
if you yourself are willing
not to go back to those
who always tell untruth.

Today, how proud I am
of the people to whom I belong,
every family, kindred and achievement —
they were not found to yield;
and although selfish individuals
are winning a prize for themselves,
Ross-Shire is triumphing,
although the landlords will not submit.

The landlords were humiliated
when they heard the news
that the poor were triumphing
whom they despised;
and that caused the landlords,
who were proud of themselves,
to promise a reward to us
if we would elect them.

Although we are proud, we were found
to be noble compared with them,
and let them give the bribes
to the people who are in their own pocket;
we will not fight for a bribe,
but we will triumph mightily;
justice is our motto,
and we will not accept the reward of lies.

A terrible judgment follows
as a reward for untruthfulness;
even Judas put his curse on it,
although his disposition was frightening;
and the man who sold the land
got a penalty after that —
he fell dead as an example,
and his sweetheart after him.

Was not that the noble fellow
whom the people followed in every step —
Greenfield, the gentleman,
who would not be deceived by bribes;
he is a very kind righteous man,
and he did not yield to toffs;
he would not take one reward from them,
as he looked up to heaven.

You know that fellow *Novar,*
with the very handsome young face;
he will not be seen in Parliament
ever representing this place;
we do not want the landlords
to be ruling in the court,
and we will not trust their words
till we see action first.

That *Novar* has an estate
and it does him no good now;
the poor are being oppressed,
they have no food for their families;
and he will not give them a drill of potatoes
to round off their meals —
and he wants in to Parliament
to stand up for us!

Note:

This poem was published in OT, April17th, 1886, where the composer is given as Murdo MacLeod, Bru, Barvas. There is a version in MacLeod 1895: 210-12, but it does not include the last two verses in the OT text, (11. 73-88).

Oran Muinntir Gheàrnaraigh

Ceud fàilt' gu muinntir Bheàrnaraigh
O bhàrd a mhuinntir Leòdhais;
Bu sibh fhèin na h-àrmainn
A bhiodh tàbhachdail sa chòmhraig;
B' e adhbhar bròin is cràdh
Gum faiceadh Pàrlamaid ur seòrsa
Gar sgiùrsadh às ur fàrdaichean,
'S ur n-àite bhith aig òisgean.

A shluagh mo chridhe, 's truagh nach mise
Bha nur measg nuair thòisich
Na coin gur ruagadh, an dùil ur fuadach
Null thar chuan bho ur n-eòlas;
Am fear a thàinig leis na bàirnigidh
Air àilgheas Dhòmhnaill,
A ghortachadh cha b' fhiach leibh e,
Ach riab sibh dheth a chòta.

'S mi bha èibhneach nuair a leugh mi
Mu ur n-èirigh còmhla,
Ri guaillibh chèile, 's rinn sin feum dhuibh —
Ghlèidh sin 'n grèim bu chòir dhuibh —
Bhon thug Sir Seumas dhuibh am feur
Bha aig ur sprèidh air mòintich;
Chan fhuadaichear neach tuilleadh dhibh
Gun fuil an cuim a dhòrtadh.

Is glan a chaidh sibh an òrdugh
Air a' mhòintich moch Di-haoine;
A-steach gu bràighe Steòrnabhaigh,
Bu bhòidheach luchd mo ghaoil-sa;
Pìob nan dos ri ceòl dhuibh,
Is gille còir cur gaoth innt',
'S mac talla bh' anns na creagan.
Ri toirt freagairt air gach taobh dhi.

Bha gach maor is siorram
'S an luchd-lagha bh' anns an àite
Air chrith le geilt nuair chunaic iad
Na curaidhean ri meàrsadh;
Gu coibhneil thug sibh cuireadh dhaibh,
'S gun cluinneadh iad mar bha sibh
Gur sàrachadh le ainneart
Aon de ainglibh dubha Shàtain.

Nuair dh'innis sibh don t-siorram
Mu na dh'fhuiling sibh de dh'fhòirneart,
'S a cheasnaich e gach fear agaibh
Mun earraid 's mun a' chòta,
Ràinig sibh am Matsonach,
Sa chaisteal san robh chòmhnaidh,
Is chuir sibh iolach suas an sin
A chual' e staigh na sheòmar.

Nuair a chunnaic e tre uinneig
Na bha muigh ga iarraidh
De threun-fhir throma dhèanadh pronnadh,
Nam bu chron bu mhiann leibh,
Thàinig agus dh'èisd e ribh,
'S am Beurla rinn sibh sgeul dha,
Mar bha sibh air ur sàrachadh
Fo làimh a dhroch fhear-riaghlaidh.

Isean salach nead na h-iolair'
Le ghob guineach millteach,
'S iomadh uan a rinn e tholladh —
'S tric am fuil air ingnean;
Ach innsidh mise dha a chunnart
Mura sguir e bhìdeadh —
Thèid a thilgeil leis a' ghunna
Shloc nach urr' e dhìreadh.

Dòmhnall dona, bronnach, brùideil,
Dòmhnall gnùgach, ciarghlas,
De Rothaich ghortach Chaile Dhubhaich —
B' olc an cliù 's an gnìomh iad;
Gus an tàinig thu do Leòdhas,
Cha robh bròg a-riamh ort —
Sgiathan fad' air ablach còta
Còmhdachadh gach sliasaid.

Sguiridh mise bhith ga leantainn;
An còrr cha chan min tràth seo;
'S e guth na tha Leòdhasaich an Glaschu,
'S tha sinn pailt an àireamh —
Mura leig e dheth a chleachdadh,
A' creachadh sluagh ar n-àite,
Thèid tri-fichead againn dhachaigh,
'S clachaidh sinn gu bàs e.

Song to the People of Bernera

A hundred salutes to the folk of Bernera
from a poet of the people of Lewis;
you really were heroes
who would be effective in the fight;
it would be a cause of sorrow and pain
if Parliament were to see the like of you
being chased out of your houses
and your place given over to ewes.

Folk of my heart, what a pity
that I was not with you, when the dogs
began to scatter you, in hope of banishing you
over the ocean away from your familiar haunts;
you did not think it was worth injuring
the ones who came with the eviction notice
at the whim of Donald,
but you tore the coat off him.

How happy I was when I read
about your rising together,
shoulder to shoulder, and it was to your advantage;
you kept the grip that you ought to hold,
since Sir James offered you the grass
that your cattle had on the moor;
not one of you will be banished again
without the blood of their body being spilt.

You went into marching order splendidly
on the moorland early on Friday;
as they marched to upper Stornoway,
my dear people were a fine sight;
the drone-pipe provided you with music
while a good lad put wind into it,
and the echo that lived in the rocks
responded to it on every side.

Every officer and sheriff
and the lawyers who were in the place
shook with fear when they saw
the heroes on the march;
you kindly gave them an invitation
so they could hear
how you were being oppressed by the tyranny
of one of Satan's black angels.

When you told the sheriff
all the oppression that you had endured,
and he had interrogated each one of you
about the messenger and the coat,
you reached Matheson
in the castle where he lived,
and you gave a great shout there
that he heard inside his chamber.

When he saw through the window
those who were seeking him,
all those heavy warriors who could crush bones,
if they had an evil intent,
he came and listened to you,
and you gave him your account in English
of how you ha been oppressed
under the hand of the bad ruler.

That dirty chick from the eagle's nest,
with his vicious, destructive beak,
tore a hole in many a lamb
and their blood was frequently on his talons;
but I will tell him of his danger,
if he does not stop his pecking —
he will be thrown down by the gun
into a pit from which he will be unable to rise.

Wicked, big-bellied, brutal Donald,
scowling, dark-grey Donald,
of the miserly Munros of Tain —
they were evil in their action and reputation —
until you came to Lewis
you never had a shoe on your foot;
long wings on a rag of coat
covered each of your thighs.

I will stop pursuing him,
and I will say no more meantime;
the voice of all the Lewismen in Glasgow —
and we are no small number — states:
If he does not give up his practice
of plundering the local population,
sixty of us will head for home
and we will stone him to death.

Note:

This poem was composed by Murdo MacLeod, "Murchadh a' Cheisteir," and the text is derived from MacLeod, 1962, 28-30.

Ceatharnaich Bheàrnaraigh

A dhaoine còire Bheàrnaraigh,
Gun òlar ur deoch-slàinte leam,
'S ged b'ann a dh'fhìon na Spàinnte,
    Gum pàigh sinn i gun sòradh.

Nuair chuala sinn ur sàrachadh,
Le bàillidh is le bàirligean,
Gur tionndadh às na fàrdaichean
    Sna dh'àraicheadh cho òg sibh.

Ge h-iomadh ùrnaigh uaigneach
Chuir ur sinnsre riamh a-suas annta,
Gum b' fheàrr le bàillidh truagh
    Bhith 'g èisdeachd nuallaich damh nan cròcan.

'S ma ghabh thu fhèin an t-ùghdarras
Na daoine còir a sgiùrsadh às,
Gun toir thu fhathast cunntas
    As do bhrùidealachd is d' fhòirneart.

Is ged chuir thu na breugan orr',
Gur daoine fiadhaich, dìomhain iad,
'S nach faighteadh car de ghnìomh asda,
    Ach iasgach 's buain na mòna,

Gun dearbh na Goill 's na Sasannaich
Gur daoine treuna, sgairteil iad,
'S gur beag a dhèanadh Machraich,
    Ann an glacaibh luchd nan clòithnean.

A shnìomhadh dhuibh ler màthraichean,
'S na nigheanan ga chàrdadh dhaibh,
'S a dh'fhigheadh anns na fàrdaichean,
    'S ga luadh le gàir nan òran.

Nuair chaidh sibh ann an òrdugh,
Le ur camain 's le ur còtaichean,
Dol suas gu baile Steòrnabhaigh,
    Bu bhòidheach leam an còmhlan.

Le pìobaire na cheannard oirbh,
A' seinn a' chiùil a b' annsa leam,
'S gun d' rinneadh riamh 's gach aimhreit leibh
   Ur nàimhdean chur air fògar.

Nuair ràinig sibh an aitreabh,
Gun dh'fhaighneachd Seumas Mathanach,
"Ciod a-nise thachair,
   Nuair tha luchd nan creach an tòir òirnn?"

Sheas fear a-mach sa champa dhibh,
'S a bhonaid gorm na làimh aige,
'S le Beurla chruaidh gun mheang
   Gun rinn e cainnt ris mar bu chòir dha:

"Bhon tha sinn fhèin 's ar sinnsireachd
Gun fhiachan no gun chìs oirnn ann,
'S do bhàillidh dubh le innleachdan
   Gar cur à tìr ar n-eòlais,

"Ma dh'innseas tu gu rianail dhuinn
An e thu fhèin a dh'iarr air e,
Gun dèan sinn mar as miannach leat,
   Mas duin' thu 's fhiach do chòta."

"Cha fhreagair dhomh 'n-diugh innse dhuibh,
Tha nì-eigin de dh'fhiamh orm,
'S sibh coltach ris na Fiantaichean,
   Nach strìochd gum faigh iad tòrachd."

Na daoine dhearbh ur còraichean,
Mo bheannachd gun robh còmhla ribh,
Na Gaidheil bhochda chòmhnadh
   Bho gach fòirneart agus dòrainn.

Beannachd leibh, a chàirdean,
Tha mi toilichte gun d' fhàgadh sibh,
'S nach deach an ruaig mar chàch oirbh
   Le bàillidh dubh gun tròcair.

The Heroes of Bernera

You good folk of Bernera,
I'll drink your health,
And even if it is in Spanish wine,
We'll pay it ungrudgingly.

We have heard of your oppression
By bailiffs and by summonses,
Turning you out of the dwellings
Where you've been reared since childhood.

Although many were the private prayers
Your ancestors uttered in them,
The wretched bailiff would rather hear
The bellowing of the horned stag.

And if you took it upon yourself
To drive the good folk out,
You will yet be called to account
For your brutality and oppression.

And although you have falsely accused them
Of being wild, indolent people,
Who could not be brought to do a hand's turn
But fishing and peat-cutting;

The Lowlanders and English will attest
That they were people of strength and vigour,
And those from the Lowland plain would be of little use
In the clutches of the folk who wore the tweed.

Tweed spun for them by their mothers -
The daughters doing the carding for them -
And woven in the houses,
And waulked with the pealing of songs.

When you took your places in order,
With your sticks and your coats,
Going up to the town of Stornoway,
Bonny was the look of the company.

You were led by a piper,
Playing the music I love best,
And in every struggle
You were able to put your enemy to flight.

When you reached the mansion,
James Matheson asked,
"What has happened, then,
When plunderers are after us?"

One of your band stood out,
His blue bonnet in his hand,
And in strong, faultless English
He appropriately addressed him:

"Our ancestors and ourselves
Have no outstanding debts or taxes,
Yet your wicked bailiff with his tricks
Is removing us from our native land;"

"If you can tell us clearly
If you personally told him to do that,
We'll do as you wish,
If you're a man worth your salt."

"It doesn't suit me to tell you today.
I'm somewhat apprehensive,
Since you look like the Fenians
Who won't give up until they raise their quarry."

The people who stood up for your rights,
My blessings upon you
For saving the poor Gaels
From all that oppression and anguish.

Goodbye, my friends,
I'm glad you've been able to stay
And not been put to flight like others
By a wicked, merciless bailiff.

Ruaig an Fhéidh

Gur moch a rinn sinn èirigh —
'S cha b' ann gun adhbhar èiginn —
A thoirt a-nuas le geur-chuims'
    Na fèidh às na mullaichean.

Di-màirt a-mach gun d' fhalbh sinn
Le brataichean 's le armachd;
Bha 'n latha soilleir sealbhach
    Mar dhearbhas sinn uile dhuibh.

Gach fear le ghunna làn-dheas
Ri aghaidh nam beann àrda,
'S nuair chìte fear na bàirich,
    Gu làr bheirte buille dha.

Mharbh sinn iad nan ceudan,
Dh'fheann sinn iad gu brèagha,
Dh'ith sinn iad gu rianail,
    Gu fialaidh 's gu cuireideach.

Chan eil sinn nar luch-reubainn,
Mar theirear leis na breugan;
'S e th' annainn daoine treuna
    Gar léireadh le uireasbhuidh.

'S iomadh latha 's bliadhna
Le bochdainn air ar riasladh
A dh'fhuirich sinn gu rianail
    Fo sheumarlain 's bhurraidhean.

Taing nan con cha d' fhuair sinn,
Bu thràillean sinn gun bhuannachd,
'S ann dh'fheumadh iad ar fuadach
    Mar ruaidh-mhadaidh buileach às.

Ar mnathan agus pàisdean
Tha nise fulang ànraidh,
An t-aodach chan eil slàn orr',
    Gach tràth iad an uireasbhuidh.

Ar dùthaich tha na fàsach
Aig fèidh is caoraich bhàna,
'S chan fhaigh sinn dhi air mhàla
    Na shàsaicheas duin' againn.

Ach moladh do an Ard-rìgh
A thiodhlaic òirnn an t-àrmunn —
'S e Dòmhnall MacRath à *Alness*
    Am martarach urramach.

'S e Dòmhnall MacRath an sàr-laoch
Nach strìochdadh do na gàrlaoich,
Ged dh'fheuch iad ris, gu cràiteach,
    'S gach àite mar b' urrainn iad.

A chailleach bheag na mòr-chùis
A their gur leatsa Leòdhas,
'S ann bhuineas i, le còir-cheart,
    Don mhòr-chuid tha fuireach innt'.

'S on fhuair sinn nis ceann-feadhna
Cha stad sinn latha no oidhche,
Gus am buannaich sinn an oighreachd
    Gu h-aoibhneach 's gu h-urramach.

Note:
Rev. Donald MacCallum, December, 1887
From *Transactions of the Gaelic Society of Inverness*, pp 360-361.

The Deer Drive

We rose early in the morning
hardship was no small reason
to bring down, with accurate aim,
the deer from the hill-tops.

We set out on Tuesday
with banners and with weapons;
the day was bright and favourable,
as we can all prove to you.

Each man with his gun loaded and ready
climbed the high hills,
and when a bellowing stag was seen,
it was struck to the ground.

We killed them in their hundreds,
we flayed them splendidly,
and we ate them in orderly fashion,
with generous portions, deftly.

We are certainly not robbers,
as is put about in lying statements;
we are, in truth, brave people
who are being ruined by poverty.

Many days and many years,
harrassed by poverty,
we have waited without disorder,
under the sway of chamberlains and fools.

We got no thanks whatever;
we were thralls who had gained nothing;
they were set upon banishing us
like foxes completely from the land.

Our wives and children
now suffer hardship:
their clothes are tattered,
and they are in need at every mealtime.

Our country is a wilderness
because of deer and white sheep,
and we cannot get enough of it on rent
to satisfy any of us.
But praise to the High King
who bestowed the hero upon us —
Donald MacRae from Alness
is the honourable martyr.

Donald MacRae was the great stalwart
who would not yield to the villains,
although they put him painfully to the test
everywhere, to the extent of their abilities.

You haughty little wifie,
who says that Lewis is your property,
it belongs by proper right
to the majority who live there.

And since we have now found a leader,
we will not cease by day or night
until we win possession of the estate
joyfully and honourably.

Note:
This poem was published in SH, December 22, 1887. Its place and date of composition are given at the foot as "Lochs, December, 1887," thus suggesting that the Rev. Donald MacCallum may have been the composer.

Spiorad a' Charthannais

O Spioraid shoilleir shàr-mhaisich,
A Spioraid ghràsmhoir chaoin,
Tha riaghladh anns an àros sin
Tha uile làn de ghaol,
Nan gabhamaid gu càirdeil riut
Gad fhàilteachadh gu caomh,
'S e siud a bheireadh àrdachadh
Do nàdar clann nan daoin'.

Nam b' eòl dhuinn thu nad mhaisealachd,
'S nam b' aithne dhuinn do luach,
'S e siud a bheireadh inntinn dhuinn
Os cionn an t-saoghail thruaigh;
Gur sona iad fhuair eòlas ort,
'S len còmhnaich thu gu buan;
'S ann tromhad tha na sòlasan
Tha 'n Tìr na Glòire shuas.

'S tu phàirticheadh gu h-èifeachdach
Rinn gnè nam flaitheas àrd,
An àite greann na h-eucorach
Bhiodh maise 's sgèimh nan gràs.
'S tu sheargadh gnè na truaillidheachd
'S a nuadhaicheadh ar càil;
'S tu thogadh chum nan neàmhan sinn
Le tarraing threun do ghràidh.

O Spioraid chaoimh nan gràsalachd,
Nam biodh tu tàmh nar còir,
'S tu dh'fhuasgladh òirnn 's a shlànaicheadh
An dream tha cnàmh fo leòn;
'S tu thogadh cridh' nam bantraichean
Gu seinn le aiteas mòr,
'S nach fàgadh gu neo-choibhneil iad
An gainntir dorch a' bhròin.

'S tu mhùchadh teine 'n naimhdeis
San t-sùil as gràinde colg;
'S tu rèiticheadh 's a chiùinicheadh
A' mhala bhrùideil dhorch;
'S tu thogadh neul na h-aingidheachd
Bharr gnùis nan aintighearn' borb,
'S a bheireadh gionach saibhreis uap'
'S gach aimhleas tha nan lorg.

'S tu bheireadh beachdan fìrinneach
Don t-sluagh mu rìoghachd nèimh;
'S tu bheireadh soisgeul fìorghlan dhuinn,
Mar dh'innseadh e bho chèin,
'S nach fagadh tu air luasgadh sinn
Le foirmean truagh nam breug,
A dhealbhadh gu h-eas-innleachdach
Tre mhìorun luchd nan creud.

Nan tigeadh saoghal dòibheartach
Gu eòlas glan ort fhèin,
'S e siud a dhèanadh sòlasach
Na slòigh tha ann gu lèir;
An sin sguireadh foill is fòirneart ann,
Is sguireadh còmhstri gheur;
Bhiodh mealltaireachd air fògradh as,
Is theicheadh neòil nam breug.

Ach 's eagal leam gu d' thrèig thu sinn,
'S do nèamh gun d' theich thu suas;
Tha daoin' air fàs cho eucorach,
'S do ghnè-sa fada uap';
Tha seiche ghreannach fèinealachd
Gan eudachadh mun cuairt;
Chan eòl dhomh aon nì reubas e
Ach saighead Dhè nan sluagh.

Ah! Shaoghail 's fada tuathail thu
On uair sin anns na thrèig
Do charthannas is d' uaisleachd thu,
'S a ghabh thu Fuath is Breug;
Mar inneal-ciùil neo-cheòlmhor dhut
Gun teud an òrdugh rèidh,
Cha seinn thu pong le òrdalachd,
'S cha deòin leat dol air ghleus.

Gun claoidhear am fear suairce leat
Tràth bhuadhaicheas fear olc;
Gun slìobar am fear suaimhneach leat,
'S gum buailear am fear gort;
Gur fial ri fear an stòrais thu,
'S gur dòit' thu ris a' bhochd;
Gur blàth ri fear a' chòmhdaich thu,
'S gur reòt' thu ris an nochdt'.

Chan eil aon nì dhut nàdarrach
Rin canar àgh air nèamh.
Chan fhaighear gnìomh gu bràth agad
Rin can an t-Ard Rìgh feum;
Ach 's leat na h-uile dìomhanas,
'S a' phian tha teachd nan dèidh;
Do dhòrainnean 's do ghàbhaidhean
Cha tàrr mi chur an cèill.

Gur leatsa neart nan aintighearnan
Is gèimhlichean nan tràill;
Gur leat guth treun nan ain-neartach,
'S guth fann an fhir tha 'n sàs;
Gur leatsa spìd is uamharrachd
An t-sluaigh tha 'n ionad àrd,
'S a mheasas cho mi-fhiùghail sinn
Ri sgùilleach air an tràigh.

Gur leat am batal dèistinneach
Le toirm a reubas cluas;
Tha glaodh a' bhàis 's na pèine ann
Gu nèamh ag èirigh suas;
Nuair thèid na prionnsan fòirneartach
Dhan spòrs an cogadh cruaidh
A chosnadh saoibhreis eucoraich
An èirig fuil an t-sluaigh.

Gur leat an togradh aimhleasach
'S na miannan teinteach caothaich
A bheir bhàrr slighe na còrach sinn,
Air seachran gòrach claon;
A dhùisgeas gaol na truaillidheachd
Is fuath do nithean naomh';
A neartaicheas 's a luathaicheas
An truaighean air clann dhaoin'.

Gur leat an creideamh buaireasach
A dhùisgeas gruaim is greann;
An creideamh nach dèan suairce sinn,
'S nach dèan ar n-uabhair fann;
An creideamh th' aig na diadhairean,
Lem miann a' chòmhstri theann:
'Nan làimh-san dh'fhàs a' Chrìosdalachd
Mar bhiasd nan iomadh ceann.

An searmonaiche prèisgeil ud,
 'S ann dh'èigheas e le sgairt
Gur malaicht' sinn mur èisdear leinn
Ra chreud-san, an tè cheart;
An àite bhith sior èigheach rinn
Mur dleasdanas 's gach beart,
A dhèanamh daoine cèillidh dhinn
An làthair Dhè nam feart.

An Crìosdaidh dubhach, gruamach ud
A chnuasaicheas gu dian,
A chuireas aghaidh chràbhach air
Mar fhàidh ann an nial,

'S e dèanamh casgairt uabhasaich
Air uamharrachd na chliabh,
Chan aithnichear air na dhèiliginn
Gun do gheill *Apolleon* riamh.

An duine caomh a dh'èireas suas
Gu nèamh air sgiath a' ghràidh,
Cha deasbair dian mu chreudan e,
'S cha bhi e beumadh chàich;
Chan Easbaigeach 's cha Chlèireach e,
Cha Ghreugach e 's cha Phàp,
Ach fear a' chridhe dhaondachail
Sam faighear gaol a' tàmh.

O Charthannais, gur h-àlainn thu,
A ghràis as àirde luach!
Ach 's lìonmhor nach toir àite dhuit
Gu bràth nan cridhe cruaidh.
Nan deònaicheadh a' cheòlraidh dhomh
Mo chomas beòil car uair,
Gun innsinn pàirt de ghnìomharan
Nam biasd thug dhutsa fuath.

Cha robh do ghnè-sa 'n Dòmhnall bochd,
Am fear bu rògaich goill,
Bha 'n dùil gum biodh gach Lèodhasach
Air fhògaradh don choill.
Ach phàigh e pàirt de dhòibheairtean,
Is gheibh e 'n còrr a thoill;
Gun aithnich e gu dòrainneach
Gur feàrr a' chòir na 'n fhoill.

Cha robh do ghnè-sa riaghladh
Ann am broilleach iarainn cruaidh
Nam bàillidhean 's nan tighearnan
Chuir sìos an tir mu thuath.
Bu charthannach na fàrdaichean
Bha seasgair, blàth innt' uair;
'S tha tìr nan daoine còire 'n diugh
Na fàsach dòbhaidh, truagh.
Gun chuir iad fo na naosgaichean
An tìr a b' aoidheil sluagh;
Gun bhuin iad cho neo-dhaontachail
Ri daoine bha cho suairc.
A chionn nach faoidte 'm bàthadh,
Chaidh an sgànradh thar a' chuain;
Bu mhios na bruid Bhàbiloin
An càradh sin a fhuair.

Gun mheas iad mar gum b' shnàthainn iad
Na còrdan gràidh bha teann
A' ceangal cridh' nan àrmann ud
Ri dùthaich àrd nam beann.
Gun tug am bròn am bàs orra
'N dèidh crabhaidh nach bu ghann,
'S an saoghal fuar gan sàrachadh,
Gun ionad blàth dhaibh ann.

A bheil neach beò san linn seo
Leis an cuimhn' an latha garbh
'S na chuireadh an cath uamhann
Waterloo nan cluaintean dearg.
Bu tapaidh buaidh nan Gàidheal ann,
Nuair dh'èirich iad fon airm;
Ri aghaidh colg nan treun-fheara,
Gun ghèill ar naimhdean garg.

Dè 'n sòlas a fhuair athraichean
Nan gaisgeach thug a' bhuaidh?
Chaidh taighean blàth a' charthannais
Nam baidealaich mun cluais;
Bha 'm macaibh anns an àraich
'S iad a' teàrnadh tìr gun truas;
Bu chianail staid am màthraichean,
'S am fàrdaichean nan gual.

Bha Breatann deanamh gàirdeachais,
Bha iadsan dèanamh caoidh.
Cha robh an tìr an àraich ac'
Na dhèanadh sgàth bhon ghaoith;
Gach fuiltean liath is luaisgean air
Le osag fhuar a' ghlinn;
Na deuraibh air an gruaidhean,
'S an fhuar-dhealt air an cinn.

A Bhreatainn, tha e nàireach dhut,
Ma dh'àirmhear ann do sgeul
Gun bhuin thu cho mi-nàdarrach
Rid fhìor-shliochd àlainn fhèin;
An tìr bha aig na gaisgich ud
A theasairg thu nad fheum,
A thionndadh gu blàr-spòrsa
Do na stròdhailich gun bheus.

Nach dìblidh cliù ar mòr-uaislean,
Na fir as neònaich mèinn?
Carson a tha iad mòr-chuiseach,
'S iad beò air spòrs gun chèill?
Nan còmhdaicheadh na ruadh-chearcan
Lem buachar uachdar slèibh,
'S e siud a b' fheàrr a chòrdadh riu
Na sràidean òir air nèamh.

O criothnaich measg do shòlasan,
Fhir fhòirneirt làidir chruaidh!
Dè 'm bàs no 'm pian a dhòirtear ort
Airson do leòn air sluagh?
'S e osnaich bhròin nam bantraichean
Tha sèid do shaoibhreis suas;
Gach cupan fion a dh'òlas tu,
'S e deòir nan ainnis thruagh.

Ged thachradh oighreachd mhòr agad,
'S ged ghèill na slòigh fod smachd,
Tha 'm bàs is laghan geur aige,
'S gum feum thu gèill da reachd.
Siud uachdaran a dh'òrdaicheas
Co-ionnan còir gach neach,
'S mar oighreachd bheir e lèine dhut,
'S dà cheum de thalamh glas.
'S e siud as deireadh suarach dhut,
Thus', fhir an uabhair mhòir,
Led shumanan 's led bhàirlinnean,
A' cumail chàich fo bhròn;
Nuair gheibh thu 'n oighreachd shàmhach ud,
Bidh d' àrdan beag gu leòr;
Cha chluinnear trod a' bhàillidh ann,
'S cha chuir maor grànd' air ròig.

'N sin molaidh a' chnuimh shnàigeach thu,
Cho tàirceach 's a bhios d' fheòil,
Nuair gheibh i air do chàradh thu
Gu sàmhach air a bòrd.
Their i, "'S e fear miath tha 'n seo,
Tha math do bhiasd nan còs,
Bhon rinn e caol na ceudan
Gus e fhèin a bhiathadh dhòmhs'."

The Spirit of Kindliness

O Spirit clear, most beautiful,
So gracious and so kind,
Who rules in that palatial place
Which love completely fills;
If we accepted you with friendliness,
And welcomed you with grace,
Surely that would elevate
The nature of our race.

If we knew you in your beauty,
And could appreciate your worth,
That would surely raise our mind
Above this piteous earth;
How happy those who know you,
With whom you ever dwell;
Through you come all the joys
Of Glory's Land above.

You would effectively impart to us
The nature of heaven's realm;
You would replace the frown of injustice
With the beauteous sheen of grace;
You would destroy corruption's nature,
And renew our true desire;
You would lift us to the heavens
With the strong pull of your love.

O gentle Spirit of graciousness!
If you lived in our midst,
You would give healing and release
To people withering with wounds;
You would inspire the hearts of widows
To sing with joyful strain,
And you would not leave them heartlessly
In the dark prison of their pain.

You would extinguish the fire of enmity
In the eye of wildest gaze;
You would pacify and quieten
The dark and brutal brow;
You would remove the look of wickedness
From the barbaric tyrants' face,
Take their greed for wealth from them
And cast treachery from its place.

You would provide for people
True views of heaven's realm;
You would give us a pure gospel,
As told in pristine state;
You would not leave us tossing
On the wretched frames of lies,
Fashioned through the deviousness
Of creed-makers' spiteful minds.

If only this world of evil deeds
Would come to know you well,
That would give to all its peoples
A joy that would excel;
Deceit and oppression then would stop
And sharp contentious strife;
Cunning tricks would be removed
And lies' dark clouds dispelled.

But I fear that you have left us
And fled to heaven above;
Our people have grown in wickedness
 Without the presence of your love;
The skin of surly selfishness
Encloaks them all around;
Nothing I know can pierce it
But the arrow of the Lord.

O World, you have gone far off course
From that hour when you lost
Your kindliness and honour,
And took to Lies and Hate;
Like a discordant instrument,
Without a string in proper tone,
You will not play an ordered note,
And you refuse to go in tune.

The kindly man is oppressed by you,
While the wicked wins the day;
The well-to-do is stroked in ease,
While the starving man is flayed;
You are generous to the wealthy,
And stingy to the poor;
You make the well-clad warmer,
And you freeze the naked's bones.

You have nothing that is natural
That heaven would call grace;
You will never produce an action
That will win the High King's praise;
You contain every form of idleness
And pain that's in its wake,
Of distresses and of horrors
Too many to relate.
To you belong oppressors' strength
And the shackles of the slaves;
You own the shout of tyrants
And the whimper of the pained;
You claim the spite and terror
Of the people who rank grand,
Who regard us as no better
Than flotsam on the sand.

The loathsome battle is your lot,
With its roar that splits the ear;
The cries of death and pain therein
Rise up to heaven's door,
When the oppressive princes
Whose sport is brutal war,
Set off to win unjust reward
In exchange for blood of poor.

To you belong the treacherous lusts
And the fiery, mad desires,
That take us from the proper path
And make us stray aside;
Which make us love corruption
And loath all holy things;
From which, with speed and certainty,
Mankind's damnation springs.

Yours too is that contentious creed
That rouses hate and ire,
The creed that will not make us kind,
And represses not our pride;
The creed beloved by those divines
Who love the sharpest strife;
Through them, Christianity has become
Like the monster of many heads.

That preachy sermoniser claims
Who shouts aloud with strength
That we are cursed if we heed not
His creed — the one that's best;
Instead of ever reminding us
Of our duty in all things,
Which would make us sensible
Before the King of Kings.

That surly, gloomy Christian
Who meditates with zeal,
Who assumes a holy countenance
Like a prophet in a trance,
Who makes a terrible slaughter
Of all horror in his breast
From his dealings you would never know,
That *Apollyon* now was dead.

The gentle man who will ascend
To heaven on love's wing
Is no contender about creeds
Nor will others feel his sting;
He is not Episcopal,
Presbyterian, Greek, or Pape,
But a man of humane heart
Whose life by love is shaped.

O Kindliness, you are beautiful
The grace of highest worth!
Yet many will never give you
A place in their hard heart.
If the Muses now would grant me
My verbal powers awhile,
I would relate some actions
Of those beasts who gave you bile.

Poor Donald knew nothing of your way,
That man of grimmest frown,
Who expected that each Lewisman
Would be exiled to the woods;
But he paid for part of his misdeeds,
And his remaining dues he'll pay;
He will realise too painfully
That justice wins the day.

Your quality did not hold sway
In that hard, iron-breasted band,
The factors and the landlords
Who oppressed the northern land;
The houses that were warm and snug
Were once filled with kindly ways,
But now that land of kindly folk
Is a poor, empty, desert waste.

They filled brim-full with snipe
The land of happy folk;
They dealt in harshest manner
With the very kindest souls;
Because they could not drown them,
They sent them fleeing overseas;
Worse than *Babylon's* captivity
Was the plight that came to these.

They reckoned as mere threads
Those cords of love that held
The hearts of those fine heroes
To the lofty land of bens;
Their grief resulted in their death,
After no lack of godly fear,
And the cold world opressed them
With no warm shelter near.

Is anyone presently alive
Who recollects that awful day,
On which was fought the fearful fight
Waterloo of bloody plains?
A fine victory was won by Gaels
When they rose in battle-arms;
Faced with the blade of bravest men,
Our fierce foes yielded fast.

What joy came to the fathers
Of those who won the fray?
The warm homes of kindliness
Towered round their ears in flames.
Their sons were on the battlefield
To save a heartless land;
Their mothers were in the saddest plight,
And their homes reduced to coal.

As Britain was rejoicing,
They were lamenting sore;
In the land that reared them,
They had no shelter from the wind
Each grey hair was being tossed
By the cold breeze of the glen;
There were tears on their cheeks,
And cold dew upon their heads.
O Britain, it is a disgrace
Should we recount your tale,
Relating how hard you dealt
With your own and truest race.
The land that those heroes had,
Who saved you in your straits,
Has now become a field of sports
For those wasters without morals.

How base the fame of our big shots,
These men of strangest sort!
Why should they stand so very high,
When they live on senseless sport?
If the grouse, with dung and droppings,
Should cover all the heather,
That is what they would prefer
To golden streets in heaven.

O tremble midst your pleasures,
You oppressor, hard and strong!
What pain or death can justly be
Your reward for people's wrongs?
The sorrowful sighs of widows
Are what inflates your wealth;
Every cup of wine you drink
Is filled with tears of dearth.

Though your estate should be so great,
And peoples yield to you,
Death has the very firmest laws,
And you will accept its rule.
That landlord will surely give
Fair dealing to all men;
Your inheritance will be a shroud
And two paces of green earth.

That will be your lowly end,
You man of great disdain,
With your notices and summonses,
Keeping others in their pain;
When you receive that quiet estate,
Your pride will greatly shrink;
 No factor there will make his strife,
Nor will officer evict.

Then the crawling worm will praise you,
For the tastiness of your flesh,
When it finds you stretched straight out
On its board without a breath;
It will say, "This one is plump,
Just right for creepy beast,
Since he made many hundreds thin
To feed himself to me."

Note:

This poem was composed by John Smith of Iarsiadar, Lewis, shortly after the Bernera Riot of 1874.

Memorial cairn at Balallan honouring the Park deer raiders.

The cairn at Gress commemorating the Back land raiders.

Will Maclean (artist) and James Crawford (stonemason) at the Aignish memorial cairn during the early stages of its construction.
Will Maclean designed the three cairns while James Crawford built them using local stone.

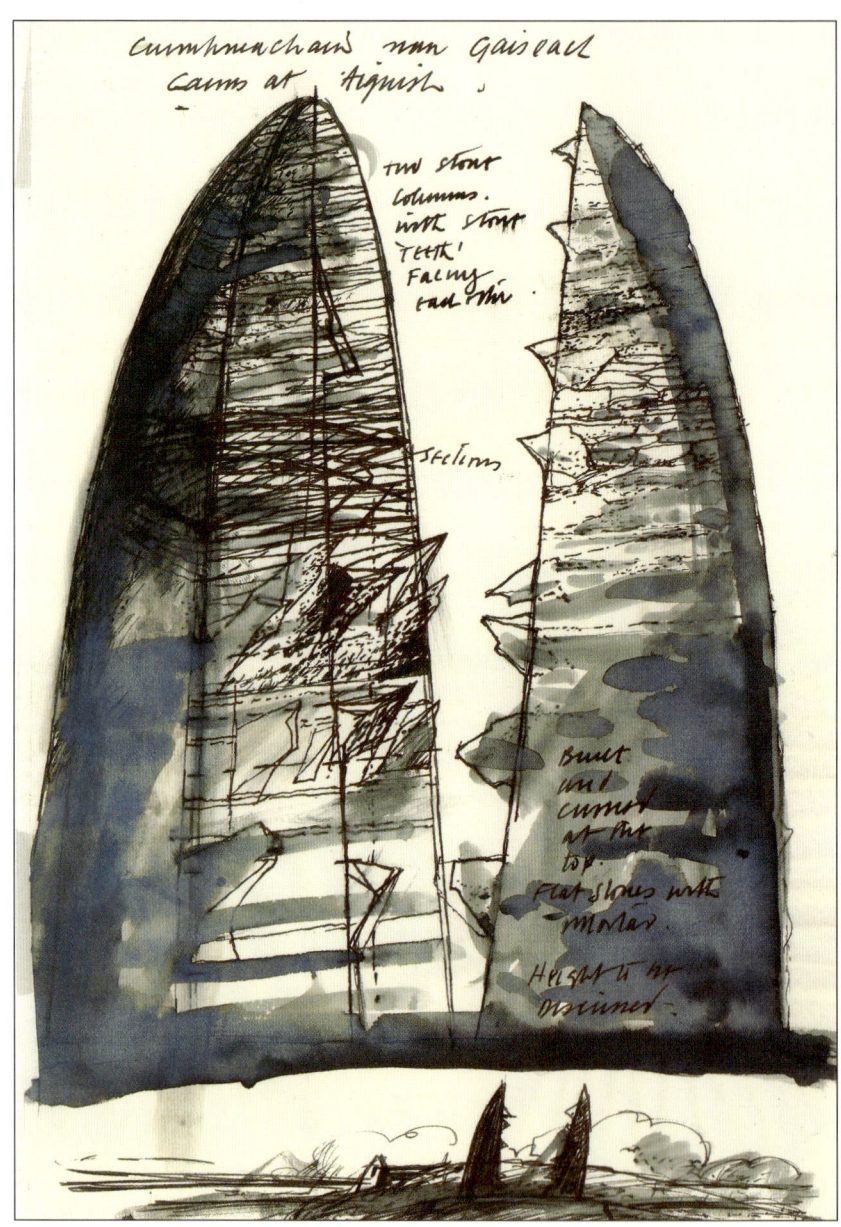

Will Maclean's sketch for the cairn at Aignish.

Ro-Radh
Aonghas MacLeòid

Chaidh am buidheann *Cuimhneachain nan Gaisgeach* a stèidheachadh anns a' bhliadhna 1989 leis an rùn gun deigheadh càirn a thogail mar chuimhneachain air na gaisgich — fireann agus boireann — anns na ceithir prìomh àitean far na chuir an sluagh am buinn an tac gus an cor is an crannchur a leasachadh.

Bha an sluagh air a bhith fada a' fulang ainneirt is fòirneirt nach bu bheag fo làmhan nan uachdaran is an riaghaltais o chionn iomadh bliadhna ach gu h-àraidh anns an naoidheamh linn deug.

Anns a' bhliadhna 1874 thachair ar-a-mach ann am Beàrnaraigh mu fhearann agus ann an 1887, thog muinntir nan Loch orra dhan Phàirc gus marbhadh na b' urrainn dhaibh dhe na fèidh aig an robh talamh gu leòr is ro bheag aca-san. Ann an 1888, bha aimhreit ann an Aignis, a-rithist mu fhearann, agus theab dòrtadh-fala dhaoine tachairt an sin. An dèidh a' Chiad Chogaidh thug muinntir Chuil is Ghriais dùbhlan don Mhorair Leverhulme agus dhleas iad còir air fearann an sin. Nach do gheall Lloyd George dhaibh gun deigheadh iad dhachaigh às a' Chogadh gu dùthaich a bhiodh freagarrach do ghaisgich gus tàmh innte le fearann gu leòr aca? Ach cha b' ann mar sin a thachair.

Nuair a chaidh *Cuimhneachain nan Gaisgeach* a chur air chois bha riochdairean às na ceithir cheàrnaidhean a tha siud air a' chiad chomataidh agus on uair sin chaidh a' chomataidh a leudachadh le buill eile a bha air leth feumail air sgàth an sgilean agus an ùidh a bha aca anns an adhbhar.

Thàinig a' Chomataidh chun a' cho-dhunaidh gu feumadh iad cuimhneachain a thogail a bhiodh cho snasail 's a ghabhadh agus a bhiodh airidh air na gaisgich a bha iad a' riochdachadh agus cuideachd feadhainn a thàlaidheadh luchd-turais a dh'amharc orra. Gus am faigheadh luchd-tadhail a-mach bun-adhbhar nan càrn, bhiodh sgrìobhadh aig gach càrn a' mìneachadh carson a chaidh a thogail.

Mar sin, chaidh sinn gu Will MacGhillEathain, dealbhadair a tha ainmeil gu nàiseanta is gu eadar-nàiseanta, agus aig a bheil ùidh mhòr ann an eachdraidh na Gàidhealtachd — tha buntanas aige ris an Eilean Sgìtheanach agus ri Leòdhas. Chruthaich esan deilbh de thoglaichean a bha iomchaidh agus tarraingeach agus snasail agus a bha a' mìneachadh nan caochladh adhbhair-aimhreit. Tha sinn fada na chomainn airson na rinn e dhuinn.

Tharraing an obair a bha seo mòran tìde agus roghnaich muinntir Bheàrnaraigh gun dealbhadh iad fhèin càrn anns an t-seann nòs, agus gun togadh iad e anns a' bhad. Rinn iad sin agus chithear an càrn seo aig ceann rathad Thòpsainn.

A bharrachd air càirn a thogail, bha e ann an rùn *Cuimhneachain nan Gaisgeach* gun deigheadh leabhar a chlò-bhualadh le eachdraidh nan tachartasan mun t-strì agus a' chòmhstri tro an tug na gaisgich buaidh gus saorsa a chosnadh dhuinne a lean nan dèidh.

Tha an euchdan air an innse le Joni Buchanan anns an leabhar seo anns a' Bheurla agus tha geàrr-eachdraidh orra anns a' Ghàidhlig leis an t-Ollamh Domhnall MacAmhlaigh, Iain MacArtair nach maireann, Iain M. MacLeòid agus Seòras Stiùbhart. Tha sinn an dòchas gu faigh sibh an leabhar seo inntinneach agus taitneach agus gun cuir an fheadhainn aig a bheil fuil nan Gàidheal a' ruith nan cuislean meas air treubhantas an sinnsearan a chuir an cath is a choisinn e.

Bha e cuideachd nar rùn gun deigheadh ionad-mìneachaidh a thogail a dh'fhoillsicheadh dòigh-beatha muinntir an eilein tro na linntean. 'S e proiseact mòr a bhiodh an seo agus fada os cionn comasan ionmhais *Cuimhneachain nan Gaisgeach*. Nach biodh e math nan deigheadh ionad den t-seòrsa seo a stèidheachadh co-cheangailte ris an sgoil choimhearsnachd a thathas an dùil a thogail air na Lochan.

Bha sinn an dòchas cuideachd gun deigheadh dealbhadh-snàidhte freagarrach a chur suas air creagan faicsinneach faisg air an rathad mhòr agus gun deigheadh co-fharpais a chur air chois gus am faigheadh sinn dealbhadh iomchaidh. Bidh sinn beò an dòchas gun tachair an dà rud a tha sin latha breàgha air choireigin.

Mar cheann-suidhe *Cuimhneachain nan Gaisgeach* bu chaomh leam taing chridheil a thoirt, às leth a' Chomataidh, do gach neach agus buidheann a thug cuideachadh agus taic-airgid dhuinn anns an oidhirp a rinn sinn gus cuimhne a chumail air gaisgeachd, treubhantas agus dìlseachd na feadhainn a chaidh romhainn.

Chaidh a' chiad trì de na sgrìobhaidhean Gàidhlig fhaicinn ann an clò an toiseach anns an leabhar *Oighreachd is Gabhaltas* a chaidh fhoillseachadh le Roinn an Fhoghlaim Cheiltich, Oilthigh Obair Dheathain, 1980.

7 Gaisgich Bheàrnaraigh 1874

An t-Ollamh Dòmhnall MacAmhlaigh

"A' chearc 's an naosg 's an coileach fraoich
Is achd a' mhaoir cho cruaidh orra
'S gur gann as urrainn duine còir
Dà bhò a bhith air buaile aige..."

(ORAN AN DIUC le Iain Chaluim Ruaidh)

Cha robh muinntir eilean Bhèarnaraigh mu mheadhan an naoidheamh linn deug gun eòlas air mì-dhòigh agus air ainneart aig amannan. A rèir an cuimhne fhèin air an eachdraidh cha bu rud annasach fear a bhith air atharrachadh às fhearann gun adhbhar na b' fheàrr na gun shaoil am maor sin iomchaidh. Bha smachd air daoine a bha teann dha-rìribh, agus bha a' mhòrchuid ga ghiùlain.

Ach bha mòran nach robh ag aontachadh leis an smachd sin, ged nach robh iad a' faicinn dòigh air a leasachadh. Agus bha fear no dithis ann a bha deònach air a dhol na bu dàine. Umhail 's gan robh daoine, bha ìre ann aig an seasadh iad an aghaidh an luchd-sàrachaidh. B' e an t-seasamh a rinn muinntir Bheàrnaraigh an aghaidh an t-siamarlain an 1874 a thog a' chiad aon dhe na còmhstrithean sin a thaobh fearainn a dh'fhàs lìonmhor anns na h-eileanan feadh an ath dhusan bliadhna.

Bha bun-adhbharan na cùise a' dol air ais a dhà no trì bhliadhnaichean. Mar dhaoine a bha fuireach an eilean mara gun mòran iathadh fearainn bha mòinteach aig muinntir Bheàrnaraigh bho shean air tìr-mhòir Leòdhais mu choinneimh an eilein. An toiseach, aig an àm air a bheil sinn a' tighinn, b' ann an àite ris an canadh iad Beinn a' Chuailein a bha a' mhòinteach aca, ach chaill iad sin an 1872 nuair a chaidh an ionad anns an robh i a dhèanamh na frìth. Na h-àite fhuair iad roinn na bu lugha de mhòintich air an robh mòinteach Iarsiadair. An lùib an atharrachaidh sa, bha e air a chur orra gàrradh a thogail air a' chrìch eadar iad fhèin agus frìth Sgealasgro — crìoch anns an robh suas ri seachd mìle a dh'fhad. Rinn iad an obair sin a thug ùine mhòr bhuapa agus a thug cothrom cosnaidh bhuapa cuideachd, air an cosgais fhèin. Chan fhaodadh iad beathach a chur air ingheilt ann gus an robh a' chrìoch dìonach.

Fhuair iad gealltanas a rèir iomraidh — agus pàipear bhon t-siamarlan ged a chaidh e 'air chall' anns an oifis aige an dèidh sin — nach deigheadh an carachadh às a' mhòintich sin fhad 's a ghiùlaineadh iad iad fhèin gu dligheach agus fhad 's a phàigheadh iad am màl na àm.

Ach cha b' ann mar sin a thachair do chroitearan Bheàrnaraigh. An dèidh na chaidh a ghealltainn dhaibh thuirt an siamarlan riutha aig deireadh 1873 — ro cheann an dà bhliadhna — nach fhaodadh iad beathach a chur gu mòinteach Iarsiadair tuilleadh. An àite na mòintich sin bha e a' dol a thoirt taca Thàcleit dhaibh agus e na bheachd Iarsiadair a thoirt do Iain Dòmhnallach, tuathanach Thàcleit. Cha robh na daoine moltach air an seo. Bha na h-uibhir de thalamh àitich an Tàcleit ach cha robh a' mhòinteach idir cho math no cho farsaing. Dh'iarr na daoine mòinteach an t-Sroim còmhla ri Tàcleit ach cha robh an Rothach deònach air an sin. Bha e air son fearann muinntir Bheàrnaraigh a chuingealachadh ris an eilean. Bheireadh na bha de thalamh àitich an Tàcleit cothrom dha air beagan de lotaichean ùra a dhèanamh do fheadhainn a bha a-staigh còmhla ri an càirdean, agus màl fhaighinn asda.

Cha robh na daoine riaraichte idir leis an seo agus dh'iarr iad lethbhreac dhen litir-aonta a bha Seumas MacRath, maor-fearainn Sgìr Uige, air a leughadh dhaibh nuair a ghabh iad a' mhòinteach, agus ris an robh iad air an ainm a chur. Cha robh an litir sa, a bha am maor-fearainn air a chur a dh'oifis an t-siamarlain, ri faotainn — bha i air a dhol 'air chall'.

'S e an ath rud a thachair gun chuir an siamarlan air a' 24mh dhen Mhàirt 1874 earraid, Cailean MacGillFhinnein, agus Seumas MacRath, am maor-fearainn, le pàipearan bàirlingidh chun an 56 croitear a bha am Beàrnaraigh, gan cur a-mach às an taighean is às an croitean agus às an còraichean mòintich an ath latha Bealltainn.

Thàinig an dithis, agus maor-cìse, no gèidsear, a bha nan cois air ceann a ghnothaich fhèin, air tìr faisg air a' chrìch eadar baile Bhriathcleit agus Circeabost (a bha, mar a bha Tàcleit, an uair sin na thuathanas), agus ghabh iad romhpa gu ceann a tuath an eilein, far an robh tromlach an t-sluaigh a' fuireach aig an àm sin am baile Bhòstadh agus am baile Thòpsann. Bha iad a' cur gille-turais romhpa gu àite mu seach ag iarraidh air daoine a thighinn cruinn air an coinneimh, agus a' toirt seachad nam pàipearan dha na croitearan nuair a ruigeadh iad. Cha b' fhada gus an robh fhios aig a h-uile duine am Beàrnaraigh air fàth an turais, agus tha e soilleir nach robhas moltach orra.

Chuir iad fios gu muinntir Thòpsann an coinneachadh faisg air taigh-sgoile a' Chnuic eadar Tòpsann agus Crothair — agus sin a' dol a ghiorrachadh an turais dhaibh. Ach cha tug iadsan feart orra. 'S ann a chruinnich iad am baile Thòpsann fhèin gus beachdachadh air dè bha dol a thachairt. Chuir sin fearg air a' mhaor-fearainn agus nuair a ràinig e fhèin agus càch am baile shuidh iad air cnoc air cùl nan taighean agus dhiùlt iad a dhol far an robh na daoine cruinn. Chronaich MacRath na croitearan bhon nach deach iad far an deach iarraidh orra. Dh'èigh e riutha gu math tàireil nach robh esan a' dol ceum an taobh a bha iad, agus gur h-iadsan a dh'fheumadh a thighinn far an robh esan. Mu dheireadh, ged a bha feadhainn ann nach robh air son gèilleadh dha chuid àrdain, dh'aontaich iad a dhol far an robh e, agus chaidh fear mu seach air adhart mar a chaidh èigheach air ainm gus an sumanadh a ghabhail.

Bha còmhradh an sin cuideachd eadar fir Thòpsann agus MacRath mu dheidhinn mòinteach Iarsiadair, agus thog iad an cùmhnant a chaidh a stèidheachadh mu a timcheall. Is esan a bha an sàs anns a' ghnothaich dhan t-siamarlan agus 's ann na làmhan a bhathas air am pàipear aonta a fhàgail. Thuirt iad gun robh e as-onarach a bhith a nise a' fiachainn ris an cùmhnant a rinneadh a bhriseadh. Ach cha d'fhuair iad èisdeachd sam bith. Dhealaich an dà bhuidheann ri chèile glè mhì-riaraichte. Bha fir Thòpsann a' faicinn gun robh iad a' dol a chall a h-uile nì a bhuineadh dhaibh le làmhachas-làidir, agus bha MacGillFhinnein agus MacRath diumbach nach d'fhuair iad am modh ris an robh dùil aca.

Nuair a dh'fhalbh iad à Tòpsann, is an gèidsear agus conastabal a' bhaile nan cois, bha e a' fàs dorcha. Bha òigridh a' bhaile air a thighinn cruinn aig a' choinneimh a dh'èisdeachd ris na bha tachairt agus lean buidheann aca iad air an t-slighe. Thòisich iad ag èigheach às an dèidh, agus an sin a' sadail chaoranan agus phloc orra. Bhuail ploc air MacGillFhinnein agus chuir seo cuthaich air. Dh'iarr e air a' chonastabal na ciontaich a chomharrachadh ach thuirt esan gun robh e ro dhorcha. Thuirt MacGillFhinnein an sin nam biodh a dhaga aigesan na chois gum biodh màthraichean am Beàrnaraigh a' gul an cuid mhac! Nuair a ràinig e Tàcleit, far na chuir iad seachad an oidhche an taigh an tuathanaich, thuirt e, a rèir cunntais, an dearbh chòmhradh a-rithist, a' cur ris nach biodh gunna as aonais an ath uair a thigeadh e; agus an ath latha, nuair a bha e a' toirt seachad nan sumanaidhean nach robh thìde aca an toirt seachad an latha roimhe sin, rinn e maoidheadh dhen aon seòrsa uair no dhà.

Chaidh am fuaim air feadh na fidhle. An ùine ghoirid bha fhios aig a h-uile duine anns an àite air na thubhairt e, agus, an ceann na bha air tachairt mu thràth, chuir e mòr-iomnaidh orra. Bha na fir a bha an sàs anns an iasgach a' dèanamh deiseil gus falbh gu muir, ach leig iad às. Thàinig iad cruinn agus thog feadhainn aca gum bu chòir a dhol an dàil MhicGillFhinnein agus iarraidh air mìneachadh dhaibh dè bu chiall dhan mhaoidheadh a rinn e; agus, 's dòcha, gealltanas fhaighinn bhuaidhe nach tilleadh e a Bheàrnaraigh a chur a chuid fhacal an cèill. Shaoil feadhainn eile gur ann bu dòcha sin a' chùis a chur na bu mhiosa. Ach mu dheireadh chuir buidheann dhe na fir òga, trì duine deug aca, romhpa gun dèanadh iad e co-dhiù. Nam beachd san cha b' urrainn do chùisean a bhith mòran na bu mhiosa na bha iad mu thràth.

Nuair a chunnaic e a' tighinn nan dàil iad, chomhairlich Murchadh Domhnallach, conastabal Bhriathcleit a bha dol leis na teachdairean chun an aisig, dhaibh a dhol dhachaigh agus gun gòraich a dhèanamh. Thuirt iad ris nach robh dùil aca olc sam bith a dhèanamh air duine agus thuirt Aonghas Thormoid ris gum faodadh esan a dhol dhachaigh nan togradh e, bhon nach b' ann ris a bha an gnothach!

Dh'fhaighnich iad de MacGillFhinnein an tuirt e na facail a bhathas a' cur às a leth, agus an ann dha-rìribh a bha e. Cha fhreagradh e an toiseach, agus an uair sin thuirt e nach ann riuthasan a thuirt e rud sam bith a thuirt e, ach ris an fheadhainn a bha a' sadail chlachan air. Agus rinn e an uair sin airson falbh. Cha robh iad riaraichte leis an sin agus rug Iain Chaluim Mhurchaidh 'c Thormoid air còta-uachdair a bha aige fo achlais, gus grèim a chumail air, agus chaidh a reubadh. Nuair a fhuair iad air stad a chur air thug iad rabhadh dha gun a leithid de mhaoidhinn a thighinn às a bheul tuilleadh agus rinn iad soilleir dha nan gabhadh e gnothach ri duine a bha anns an àite, le gunna no gun ghunna, gum biodh ceannach aige air. B' iad Iain Chaluim, Aonghas Thormoid agus Tormod Mhurchaidh 'c Amhlaigh an triùir a bha air thoiseach anns a' chùis.

Nuair a fhuair MacGillFhinnein a chasan às cha b' fhada gus an do thòisich e ag innse mar a bheireadh e fir Bheàrnaraigh dhan lagh bhon a ghabh iad gnothach ris, agus e a' riochdachadh an lagha nam measg. Nuair a ràinig e Steòrnabhagh sgaoil e an uirsgeul agus chuir e conastabail a' bhaile nan earail mun chunnart a bha am fir Bheàrnaraigh.

Cealla-deug an dèidh dhan seo tachairt, air an 8mh latha den Ghiblein, chaidh Aonghas Thormoid a Steòrnabhagh air cheann turais. Chunnaic MacRath an sin e agus chomharraich e do MacGillFhinnein e. Chaidh esan a dh'innse dha na poileis gun robh fear dhe na reubaltaich nam measg agus sheall e dhaibh cò e.

Chaidh dithis dhe na poileis gus a chur an sàs agus a thoirt dhan phrìosan, ach dhiùlt e gèilleadh dhaibh agus bhon a bha e na dhuine calma cha deach aca air a chur an grèim an toiseach idir, agus chuir iad a dh'iarraidh cuideachadh. Tharraing a' chòmhstrì daoine a choimhead dè a bha a' tachairt. Thuirt Aonghas riutha gun robhas ga chur an sàs is gun e air eucoir sam bith a dhèanamh agus a dh'aindeoin 's gun gheall e gun tigeadh e gu cùirt latha sam bith a chuireadh iad roimhe. Chaidh an sluagh a bha timcheall an lìonmhorachd agus bhrùth iad a-steach gu dùmhail timcheall air na poileis, a bha a nise a' slaodadh Aonghais dhan phrìosan, air dhòigh agus nach b' urrainn dhaibh a dhol air adhart. Agus gu dearbha chaidh feadhainn aca anns na h-eadraigean a' fiachainn ri Aonghas a thoirt saor. Chaidh Iain Mac a' Ghobhainn, a bha ris a' bhèicearachd, e fhèin a chur an sàs airson a dhìchill anns a' chùis.

Chuir sin am mì-rian na bu mhiosa buileach agus tha e follaiseachadh nach robh an sluagh deònach air sgaoileadh. Thàinig procadairean a' bhaile a shealltainn air an tuasaid, agus nuair nach tugadh feart orrasan chaidh fios a chur air an t-siorramh. Bho dheireadh leugh esan **Achd na h-Aimhreite** agus chaidh an sluagh mu sgaoil, ged nach b' ann air an dòigh. Thugadh Aonghas, agus am fear a chaidh anns na h-eadraigean air a thaobh, dhan phrìosan. Fhad 's a bha Aonghas an sin an grèim aig na poileis, thug MacGillFhinnein ionnsaidh air agus chaidh a mhilleadh is gun chothrom aige air e fhèin a dhìon.

Chaidh an naidheachd air ais a Bheàrnaraigh far nach do ghabhadh rithe le ciùineas. Chuir muinntir an eilein romhpa mura faigheadh e às a' phrìosan gun deigheadh iad a Steòrnabhagh iad fhèin ga leigeil mu sgaoil. Chaidh am fios mun cuairt agus dh'ullaich gach fear anns an eilean a bha air a chothrom e fhèin airson an turais. Bha crann eathair aca deiseil gus am prìosan a bhriseadh nan tigeadh e gu ìre sin a dhèanamh. Dh'fhalbh iad a Steòrnabhagh is pìobaire air an ceann, iad fhèin agus feadhainn à àiteachan timcheall a bha deònach air an cuideachadh gus an còraichean a sheasamh. Chualas gun robh iad air an t-slighe agus chaidh Aonghas a leigeil às agus thachair e riutha air taobh a-muigh a' bhaile.

Ach cha do leig iad às an turas. Bha iomnaidh orra mun t-sumanadh a fhuair iad a bha a' toirt an cuid thaighean is an cuid chroitean bhuapa. Cha robh earbsa sam bith aca às an t-siamarlan agus chuir iad romhpa gun deigheadh iad agus gun iarradh iad còmhradh air an uachdaran gus an innseadh iad dha cho doirbh agus a bha an cor agus gus an cuireadh iad na shùilean an dleasdanas a bha air dhe an taobh.

Ràinig iad am baile agus bhathas caran iomaganach romhpa an sin, gun fhios dè a dhèanadh iad nuair a ruigeadh iad. Ghabh iad a null gus an do ràinig iad aitreabh an uachdarain, chruinnich iad air an lianaig air beulaibh an taighe, agus chaidh fear aca chun an dorais a dh'iarraidh còmhradh air an uachdaran. Fhuair iad sin agus dh'innis iad dha mar a bha air tachairt riutha fo làmhan an t-siamarlain. Ghuidh iad air an staid a leasachadh air neo gum biodh iad air am fàgail gun dìon is gun seilbh. Gheall esan gun dèanadh e rannsachadh mu dheidhinn na cùise, oir nach robh lorg aige air dè a bha am beachd a shiamarlain a dhèanamh. Nuair a fhuair fir Bheàrnaraigh an gealladh sin chaidh iad air ais dhachaigh sìobhalta gu leòr. Ach cha b' fhada mus tàinig a thoradh am follais. Cha deachaidh na sumanaidhean a chasg — gu dearbh 's ann a chaidh seulachadh an lagha orra — agus cha d'fhuair na daoine cobhair an dòigh sam bith gus an robh e follaiseach do Shir Seumas gum biodh e na fhàbhar fhèin a bhith na bu shoitheamh riutha.

'S e an ath thionndadh a bha anns a' chùis gun deachaidh Aonghas Thormoid, a chaidh a ghlacadh an Steòrnabhagh, Iain Chaluim a reub còta MhicGillFhinnein nuair a chaidheas timcheall air am Beàrnaraigh, agus Tormod Mhurchaidh 'c Amhlaigh a bha air thoiseach anns an obair sin cuideachd, a ghairm gu cùirt an Steòrnabhagh deireadh an t-samhraidh.

Chaidh a' chùirt a chumail air an t-17mh dhen Iuchair 1874. Chaidh na prìosanaich a ghairm agus na bhathas a' cur às an leth a leughadh — 's e sin gun robh iad air ionnsaigh ghamhlasach agus an-dligheach a thoirt air Cailean MacGillFhinnein air a' 25mh dhen Ghiblein eadar baile Briathcleit agus crìoch Chirceaboist, air a dhol mun cuairt air ann an dòigh iorghaileach agus gharg, air breith air bhroilleach agus air choileir air agus air beantainn ri roinnean eile dhe phearsa, agus air maoidheadh a mharbhadh; air a dhraghadh agus air a bhruthadh, agus air a chòta-uachdair is a leigeans a reubadh; agus, mar sin, air eagal a bheatha a chur air agus air a leòn na cholainn; gun rinn iad sin agus fhios aca gur h-e oifigeach lagha a bha ann, agus gur h-ann a rinn iad e mar dhìoghaltas air airson gun choimhlion e a dhleasdanas mar oifigeach lagha. Chaidh fhaighneachd dhe na prìosanaich an robh no nach robh iad ciontach agus fhreagair iad nach robh. Mar sin chaidh luchd-breithe a thaghadh agus chaidh an dearbhadh air adhart.

Ghairm Uilleam Ros, am procadair, air luchd-fianaise an aghaidh nam prìosanach agus dh'innis iadsan an taobh fhèin dhen t-seanchas. 'S e a' chiad fhear a ghairm e Domhnall Munro an siamarlan. Dhaighnich esan dha gun robh e air MacGillFhinnein fhasdadh mar earraid, agus gur e na sumanaidhean leis an robh e air a chur a-mach a bha fo chomhair na cùirte, agus gun robh iad air an coilionadh gu dligheil.

B' e Teàrlach Innis fear-lagha à Inbhir Nis a bha a' tagradh cùis nam prìosanach. 'S e a' chiad dòigh a ghabh e air an seo ionnsaigh làidir a thoirt air fianaisean a' phrocadair. Na ath-cheasnachadh air an t-siamarlan sheall e glè shoilleir dè an seòrsa duine a bha ann dheth. Sheall e gun robh e an sàs anns gach rud a bha a' dol anns an àite, bhon mhailisi gu bòrd nam bochd, fhad 's a bheireadh e buannachd dha fhèin às. Sheall e gun robh e a' saoilsinn gun robh croitearan gun fhiù, nach robh e dhen bheachd gun robh iad airidh air còraichean na dìon sam bith, agus nach robh dàil sam bith gu bhith ann gan atharrachadh às an àite nan robh prothaid ri thoirt às an atharrachadh. Chuir an Rothach an aghaidh feadhainn dhe na ceistean, agus dhiùlt e feadhainn aca a fhreagairt (ged nach do leig an siorramh sin leis ach ainneamh) ag ràdh nach robh gnothach aca ris a' chùis a bha fo chomhair na cùirte. Ach bha e follaiseach gun robh Innes ag obair air raon na b' fharsainge, gus dealbh iomlan dhen chùis a chuir fir Bheàrnaraigh gu boil a shealltainn dhan luchd-breithe, feuch an tuigeadh iad brìgh na h-iomnaidh a chuir gluasad orra gus a dhol an dàil MhicGillFhinnein.

Nuair a chaidh MacGillFhinnein fhèin a ghairm cha deachaidh leis càil na b' fheàrr. Rinneadh soilleir gun robh e air am maoidheadh a chuireadh às a leth a dhèanamh. Bha a fhreagairtean cùilteach air iomadh cuspair ach cha b' urrainn dha a dhol às àicheadh gur h-e MacRath a chomharraich Aonghas Thormoid dha an Steòrnabhagh an latha a chuir e na poileis an sàs ann — nach do dh'aithnich e e.

A' ceasnachadh MhicRath fhuair Innes bhuaidhe gun robh MacGillFhinnein air am maoidheadh a dhèanamh dha-rìribh, barrachd air aon uair. Fhuair e bhuaidhe cuideachd nach do mhaoidh duine air MacGillFhinnein gun deigheadh a mharbhadh nan tilleadh e air ais a Bheàrnaraigh. Ach thuirt e gun tuirt cuideigin gur h-ann lomnochd a dheigheadh e dhachaigh nan gabhadh e air a thighinn air ais, agus thuirt e gun robh e dhen bheachd gun robh MacGillFhinnein anns na h-uibhir de chunnart.

Dh'innis Pàdraig Bàn, an gèidsear, fhiosrachadh fhèin air na thachair, agus bha e follaiseach gun robh a shealladh san mòran na b' fhàbharaiche dha na prìosanaich. Dhaighnich e gun robh an earraid air a radha nan robh a ghunna aigesan gum biodh màthraichean am Beàrnaraigh air a bhith gul an cuid gineil, agus gun tug e tionndadh air an aon chùis uair is uair an oidhche sin agus an ath latha. Thuirt e gur e seo a bha air aire nam fear a chuir stad orra air an t-slighe chun an aisig, nach deachaidh facal a radha an sin mu dheidhinn nan sumanaidhean agus nach b' e sin a chuir air an t-slighe iad idir. Thuirt e cuideachd nach do mhaoidh duine air beatha MhicGillFhinnein, ach gur h-ann a thuirt fear aca (na bheachd san Aonghas Thormoid) ris gun eagal a bhith air oir nach robh e nan rùn olc sam bith a dhèanamh air. Dh'innis e mar a bha gamhlas mòr an sàs am MacGillFhinnein a thaobh mar a thachair ris, agus mar a bha e a' cur roimhe dìoghaltas a dhèanamh. Thuirt e cuideachd gun robh MacRath tàireil ris na daoine an Tòpsann agus gur beag an t-iongnadh ged a bhiodh fearg ag èiridh orra, a' faighinn a leithid de achmhasan agus am màl pàighte aca gu cothromach. 'S e mar a thachair an sin a thug air an òigridh an leantainn agus dùbhlan a thoirt dhaibh nuair a dh'fhalbh iad air an t-slighe a Thàcleit.

Nuair a chrìochnaich am procadair, ghairm Innes fianaisean as leth nam prìosanach. Bha an triùir fhear deug a bha air stad a chuir air an earraid aige an làthair agus bha e deiseil gus an gairm fear mu seach, ach an dèidh dhan trìtheamh fear fianais a thogail thuirt ceannard an luchd-breithe ris nach ruigeadh e a leas an còrr aca a ghairm. Dh'aontaich e leis an sin ach ghairm e air dithis a dhaighnich gun dh'aithris MacGillFhinnein a mhaoidheadh a thaobh a ghunna riuthasan nuair a chaidh e thuca le an sumanaidhean air madainn Diardaoin air a shlighe air ais chun an aisig. Chuir sin crìoch air na fianaisean. Thuirt am procadair bhon a bha e cho anmoch (deich uairean feasgar) nach robh e a' dol a chosg tìde ag radha a' chorra riutha. Thuirt e gun robh ciont nam prìosanach follaiseach agus dh'iarr e air an luchd-breithe an dìteadh air a h-uile puing.

Ach a dh'aindeoin cho anmoch 's a bha e rinn Innes òraid fhada a' cur an cèill an t-seallaidh sin air a' ghnothaich a bha e air a bhith a' cur an sùilean an luchd-breithe fad na h-ùine. Sheall e dhaibh ainneart agus an-iochd an t-siamarlain agus, air a' cheann thall, an as-onair leis na rinn e gnothach ri fir Bheàrnaraigh. Sheall e dhaibh cho tàireil agus a bha am maor-fearainn riutha. Sheall e gu sònraichte mar a bha MacGillFhinnein air a ghonadh leis an as-urram a shaoil e a fhuair e bhuapa; mar a thug seo air maoidheadh orra uair agus uair. Rinn e follaiseach gur h-e an iomnaidh a chuir sin orra a thug orra dhol na dhàil, agus, nuair a rinn iad sin, nach robh càil fainear dhaibh ach dèanamh cinnteach nach cuireadh e a mhaoidheadh an cèill. Mar sin cha do bhean iad ri a phearsa ged a thug iad rabhadh dha mu ghnìomharan.

Sheall e gur h-e an gamhlas a dhùisg sin ann agus miann an dìoghaltais a bu choireach gun chuir e na poileis an sàs an Aonghas Thormoid, agus gur h-e sin agus nach b'e ciont nam prìosanach a dh'fhàg gun robh iad anns a' chùirt. Thuirt e nach robh de dh'adhbhar an aghaidh nam prìosanach ach an seanchas a rinn MacGillFhinnein air a' chùis, seanchas nach robh comhaonta dhuine sam bith eile ri mòran dheth. Thuirt e gur e an sgeul a chuir e fhèin fo an comhair an fhìrinn, agus gun robh e cinnteach gun tigeadh iad gu an co-dhùnadh air a' bhunait sin, agus nach tugadh iad àite sam bith a dh'aon chuid dha na bhiodh iad a' saoilsinn a chòrdadh ri urrachan mòra an eilein no dhan iomairt gun stàth a bha iad air fhaicinn anns na pàipearan-naidheachd air an ràithe chaidh seachad.

An uair sin rinn an siorramh òraid co-dhùnaidh a bha gu math cothromach a' cur dà thaobh na cùise fo an comhair agus a' mìneachadh an lagha dhaibh a thaobh na binn a bu chòir dhaibh a thoirt a-mach — a rèir is dè an taobh a chreideadh iad.

Bha an sluagh cho dùmhail anns a' chùirt agus nach fhaigheadh an luchd-breithe air ais dhan t-seòmar a bha air a chur air leth dhaibh, agus thàinig orra an dearbhadh a dhèanamh far an robh iad. An ceann ùine ghoirid thàinig an Ceannard aca air adhart leis a' bhinn uile-aontach gun robh na prìosanaich uile neochiontach.

An làrna-mhàireach anns a' mhadainn chaidh am fear a bha air a dhol anns na h-eadraigean gus Aonghas Thormoid a thoirt saor bho na poileis a thoirt air beulaibh na cùirte airson a chompàirt anns an tuasaid sin, ach fhuair esan saor cuideachd. Cha d'fhuaras air a' chasaid a bha na aghaidh a dhearbhadh.

An dèidh sin chaidh Cailean MacGillFhinnein, e fhèin, a shumanadh agus cur às a leth gun rinn e ionnsaidh an-dligheach air Aonghas Thormoid: gun bhuail agus gun bhreab e e nuair a bha e an sàs aig na poileis ann an Steòrnabhagh. Cha deachaidh cho math leis-san agus a chaidh le càch oir thug a' mhòr-chuid dhen luchd-breithe a-mach binn gun robh e ciontach. Ach ghuidh iad a' Chùirt a bhith iochdmhor ris, agus cha deach air ach càin fichead tasdan no deich latha anns a' phrìosan. Chaidh a' chàin a phàigheadh.

Bha an dà latha sin, an 7mh agus an t-8mh latha dhen Iuchair 1874 cudthromach chan ann a-mhàin an eachdraidh fir Bheàrnaraigh ach an eachdraidh chroitearan gu h-iomlan. Sheall iad, 's dòcha a' chiad uair, gum faodadh croitearan an còraichean a sheasamh gun an lagh an dìteadh airson sin a dhèanamh. Thug seo misneachd dhaibh a bha a dhìth orra gu mòr.

Sheall iad cuideachd nach robh aon chuid maor no earraid no siamarlan os cionn an lagha, fhad 's a bha an lagh cothromach agus fhad 's a bha tagraichean ann a bha a' sireadh ceartais. Dh'fhàg a' chùirt MacGillFhinnein gun chliù agus chan fhacas mòran dhe an Leòdhas an dèidh sin. A thaobh an t-siamarlain dheth, rinn a' chùirt follaiseach dha na h-uile cho suarach 's a bha e a' cur nan daoine a bha fo a mhaorsainneachd — dhearbh e sin le a bhriathran fhèin. Rinn e follaiseach cuideachd a' ghionachd agus an t-àrdan leis an robh e a' dol an sàs na chuid obrach, gach cuid dha fhèin agus dhan uachdaran, a mhaighistir. Dh'fhàg a' chùirt esan gun mòran de chliù cuideachd agus cha do mhair e fada anns a' mhaorsainneachd as a dèidh. Chaidh mòran a radha gus an t-uachdaran a thoirt saor às a' chùis, ged a tha e follaiseach dhuinn an-diugh gun robh e mòran na b' fhillte innte na chuireadh às a leth. Fhuair esan às na bu shaoire na càch.

A thaobh croitearan Bheàrnaraigh dheth, cha deach an cur às an fhearann no às a' mhòintich a bha aca air tìr-mhòr Leòdhais agus tha e soilleir gun robhas na bu shoitheamh riutha anns na bliadhnaichean an dèidh na cùirte. Chaidh ath-roinn a dhèanamh air an eilean agus chaidh Circeabost, an 1878, agus an uair sin Tàcleit, an 1880, a chur fo dhaoine, an uair a thàinig an gabhaltas tuathanais gu crìch. Bha a' mhòine gu lèir air caitheamh am Bòstadh, agus an Tòpsann bha an sluagh air fàs cho lìonmhor agus nach cumadh an t-àite e. Chan eil teagamh nach e an seasamh a rinn iad airson an còraichean agus a' bhuaidh a bha leis an t-seasamh sin a choisinn am faothachadh sin dhaibh. Ach, mar chroitearan eile, thàinig orra fuireach ri Achd nan Croitearan gus còraichean riaghailteach a bhuileachadh orra. 'S e a' bhuaidh a bha aig an seasamh air inntinn dhaoine, agus air a' ghluasad a dh'adhbharaich gun deach an Coimisean bhon tàinig an Achd a chur air chois anns a' chiad àite, a tha a' dleasadh àite dhaibh ann an eachdraidh an dùthcha. Thogadh càrn cuimhne orra am Beàrnaraigh an 1992.

8 Reud na Pàirce 1887

Ian M. Macleòid

Bha cor a' Ghàidheil, cor an Leòdhasaich agus cor Mac nan Loch gu h-àraidh glé ànradhach anns an leth mu dheireadh den naodhamh linn deug. Aon uair is gun dhearbh am fiadh is a' chaora gu robh iad na bu bhuannachdail don uachdaran na bha an croitear, chaidh esan a shàrachadh anns a h-uile dòigh a ghabhadh dèanamh gus fhuadach gu tìrean cèin no gu àitichean mì-thorrach far nach soirbhicheadh a' chaora no am fiadh. Tha fhios aig a h-uile duine mar a chaidh Dùthaich MhicAoidh fhàsachadh agus mar a rinn an trusdar Pàdruig Sellar fòirneirt air an t-sluagh. Bha trusdaran ann an Leòdhas cuideachd a bha a' dèanamh geur-leanmhainn air na daoine agus 's e an seumarlan Dòmhnall Rothach am fear bu mhiosa dhiubh. Sgrìobh Iain mac a' Ghobhainn, no Iain Phàdraig à Iarsiadar mu dheidhinn-san:

'N sin molaidh a' chnuimh shnàigeach thu
Cho tàirceach 's a bhios d' fheòil,
Nuair gheibh i air do chàradh thu
Gu sàmhach air a bòrd.
Their i, "'S e fear miath tha 'n seo,
Tha math do bhiasd nan còs,
Bhon rinn e caol na ceudan
Gus e fhèin a bhiathadh dhòmhs'."

Air na Lochan ann an Leòdhas tha talamh mòr na Pàirce, far an robh mòran sluaigh ri còmhnaidh aig aon àm. Bha dà cheud ann an Calbost ann an 1911; chan eil ann an diugh ach ceathrar (1978). Mar a thuirt Murchadh Mac a' Ghobhainn, am bàrd à Liùrbost:

B' èiginn dhaibh an cùl a chur
Ri slèibh is glinn an dùthchais
Airson gum biodh na stùcannan
Nan lùchairt chaorach mhòra.

Tha na slèibh a dh'àraicheadh
An treubh a ghleusadh stàilinnean
An diugh fo fhèidh nam fàsaichean
'S fo chaoraich bhàna bhòidheach.

Cha robh ach dà sgìre ann an Eilean Leòdhais an toiseach - Sgìre na h-Uidhe agus

Sgìre Bharbhais. Bha am fearann ris an canar an diugh na Lochan ann an Sgìre na h-Uidhe agus cha robh mòran sluaigh air thaigheadas ann - gu h-àraidh air taobh deas Loch Eireasord. Ann an làithean Chlann 'ic Leòid bha e air a cheadachadh do na h-Uigich a bhith a' dol don Phàirc leis an sprèidh aca agus tha geàrraidh air taobh deas Loch Sìphort, faisg air an t-Sruth, ris an canar Airigh Dhòmhnaill Chaim. Is ann an seo a chaidh e air falach, tha e coltach, an uair a bha na Tàilich ga lorg ann an Uig. Nuair a fhuair Clann Choinnich grèim air Leòdhas ann an 1610 is ann aig Ceann Loch Sìphort a thog iad a' chiad chaisteal - tha an tobhta ri faicinn fhathast - agus 's ann fo ainm an àite seo a ghabh Cailean, a' chiad Iarla, an tiotal aige. Thog iad gàrradh eadar Loch Sìphort agus Loch Eireasord airson na fèidh a chumail a-staigh agus na poidsearan a chumail a-muigh. 'S e Gàrradh an Tighearna an t-ainm a bha air, agus tha an làrach aige-san ri fhaicinn fhathast cuideachd.

Ann an 1716 's e aon duine a bha a' pàigheadh màil anns a' Phàirc, Alasdair MacCoinnich ann an Tàbost, duine a bha càirdeach don uachdaran, ach mu 1800 bha daoine air a dhol air thaigheadas ann an Sìldinis, Isginn, Stìomrabhagh, Leumrabhagh agus an Orasaidh. Chaidh a' Phàirc a thoirt air mhàl aig toiseach an naodhamh linn deug do Lachlainn MacFhionghuin à Corraidh anns an Eilean Sgìtheanach agus an dèidh sin do Dhòmhnull Stiùbhart agus a bhràithrean à Peart, sìos gu 1842. An dèidh sin chaidh a' Phàirc a chumail mar thaca chaorach le atharrachadh thuathanach gus a' bhliadhna 1883 nuair a leig Pàdruig Mòr Sellar seachad i. Ann an 1831 bha seachd croitearan ann an Sìldinis, sia-deug ann an Isginn, seachd-deug ann an Orasaidh, fichead ann an Leumrabhagh agus ochd ann an Stìomrabhagh - 's ann aig na Stiùbhartaich a bha a' Phàirc aig an àm seo.

Chaidh croitearan Isginn a ruagadh ann an 1833, croitearan Orasaidh agus Shìldinis ann an 1838 agus feadhainn Leumrabhaigh ann an 1841. Chaidh trì fichead croitear a ruagadh gu lèir, agus chaidh cuid dhiubh gu tìrean cèin, seachd air fhichead a Chrosbost, feadhainn a Thunga is a Tholstadh agus feadhainn a Steòrnabhagh. Eadar 1883 agus 1886 cha robhas a' lorg neach a ghabhadh a' Phàirc air mhàl agus chuir mòran de mhuinntir nan Loch tagraidhean chun na Mnatha-uasail NicMhathain feuch an toireadh i dhaibh pàirt de thalamh na Pàirce air mhàl; cha do rinn ise fiù 's am freagairt.

Ghabh Mgr. Iòsaph Platt a' Phàirc air mhàl anns a' bhliadhna 1886, bliadhna ro Chreach Mhòr nam Fiadh, agus ged a sgrìobh an t-Urramach Dòmhnall MacCaluim ceithir rainn deug de dh'òran a' cur sìos air 'Bodach Isgin', mar a bha aige air, bha Mgr. Platt, agus gu h-àraidh a bhean, glè mheasail aig a' mhòr-shluagh san àite; 's e 'Lady Platt' a bha aca oirre-se. Seo dhà de rainn MhicCaluim:

Ceann Loch Eireasord.

'Tha mise rìoghchadh cho fad 's a chì mi,'
Thuirt Bodach Isgin, 'thar monadh 's cruach,'
'S gun d' thuirt e 'n fhìrinn 's e bhris mo chrìdh-sa
'S a dh'fhàg an tìr seo air chrith le fuachd.

'A-mach o 'n Airigh 's an robh na h-àrmainn
A' gabhail tràth air mo bhradan 's m' fhiadh
Gu ruig a Chàbhaig tha tìr na Pàirce
Fo 'm chois na fhàsach 's le m' iuchair gléight.'

Anns na bliadhnaichean ro Achd nan Croitearan (1886) bha bochdainn mhòr ann am measg an t-sluaigh agus b' e aon adhbhar air an seo gu robh an t-uachdaran a' leagail màil ro-throm air a' chroitear. Dhearbhadh seo an uair a rinn Coimisean nan Croitearan sgrùdadh air màil ann an Leòdhas agus a lùghdaich iad mòran dhiubh. Bha timcheall air dà fhichead a bha dhà uiread 's bu chòir dhaibh, agus ann am fichead eile gheàrr an Coimisean iad mar a leanas: 52.5, 53, 54.5, 55, 55.5 (ceithir), 59 (dhà), 59.25, 59.5, 60, 61, 61.25, 62.75%. Ann an Airigh-Bhruthaich bha aon chroit air an deach am màl a lùghdachadh gu ìre 66.6%. Mar sin cha leig duine sam bith a leas a ràdh gu robh an t-uachdaran math do na croitearan ann an Leòdhas - 's ann a bha e a' feuchainn ris a h-uile sgillinn a b' urrainn dha a thoirt uapa.

Aig an àm seo bha maighistir-sgoile comasach ann am Bail-Ailean - fear Dòmhnall MacRath. Bhuineadh e do Chaol Loch Ailse.

Bha e na fhear-stiùiridh is na fhear-cuideachaidh do na croitearan. Is iomadh croit a thomhais e do chroitearan a bha a' dol mu choinneamh a' Choimisein - agus bhiodh coinneamhan tric anns an sgoil far am biodh na croitearan a' cruinneachadh agus a' meòrachadh agus a' deasbad mu dhòighean air an crannchur a leasachadh.

Anns a' bhliadhna 1887 bha droch Fhoghar ann agus bha mòran den bhuntàta lobhte, agus bha muinntir nan Loch air an tolladh leis an acras. Mar sin chaidh aontachadh aig coinneamh ann am Bail-Ailean air an aonamh latha deug den t-Samhain, 1887, gun deidheadh oidhirp a dhèanamh gus cor an t-sluaigh a thoirt fo chomhair an Riaghaltais, agus gur h-e an dòigh a b' fheàrr air seo a dhèanamh gun deidheadh a h-uile duine ann an sgìre nan Loch, aig an robh an cothrom, don Phàirc air latha sònraichte agus gu marbhadh iad na b' urrainn dhaibh de na fèidh.

'S e Dimàirt an 22mh latha den t-Samhain an latha a chaidh a thaghadh gus a dhol don Phàirc. Chaidh fios a chur gu oifis a' phàipear-naidheachd, *North British Daily Mail* agus thàinig fear-naidheachd air a' bhàta oidhche Dhiciadain.

Dithis ghaisgeach às a' Phàirc nuair a bha iad na bu shine: Alasdair MacPhàrlain, 10 Marbhaig, (gu h-àird) agus Seòras Iain, 14 Marbhaig.

Air madainn Dimàirt, nuair a chruinnich an sluagh gu lèir aig Feiriseal, choisich iad a-steach don fhrìth mar arm, ceathrar anns gach sreath, agus nuair a bha iad trì no ceithir cheud slat a-staigh, stad iad agus chaidh cùisean a chur ann an òrdugh. Chaidh cuid a thaghadh airson stàcadh, cuid airson nan cabraichean is nan seann sheòl is nam praisean agus ghnothaichean eile a bha aca a ghiùlain, agus cuid eile airson closaichean nam fiadh a thoirt chun a' champa aig Airidh Dhòmhnaill Chaim. B' e an fheadhainn aig an robh na gunnaichean na sealgairean.

Mu mheadhan latha Dimàirt, bha Sandaidh MacPhàrlain, no Alasdair Beag Alasdair Thormoid à Marbhaig, còmhla ri grunnan eile thall aig Loch Brollum nuair a thàinig eathar air tìr le Dùbhghlas Thorneycroft, am bràthair a b' òige a bh' aig a' Bhean-uasal Platt. Bha na croitearan a' bruidhinn ris fhèin is ris na gilidhean nuair a dh'fhosgail fear de na gilidhean bascaid bidhe a bha nan cois. "An ainm Sealbh nach roinn thu am biadh sin nar measg gu lèir!" arsa Sandaidh MacPhàrlain. Rinneadh sin agus chaidh drama a thairgse do na croitearan cuideachd.

Air feasgair Dimàirt, chaidh cuid de na fèidh fheannadh agus chaidh an fheòil a ghearradh na staoigean deiseil airson a bruich, ach chaidh aon damh fhàgail slàn airson a ròsdadh.

Mar a thuirt cuideigin:

Aig Airigh Dhòmhnaill Chaim
Rinn sinn camp 's bha teine againn
'S bha fear na bèine deirg
'S na coise fada fannachadh.

Ghabh bodach còir feusagach, Alasdair Thormoid à Marbhaig, an t-altachadh. Le a chùlaibh ris na teinntean thog e a làmhan os a chionn agus thuirt e gur h-e latha mòr a bha siud ann an eachdraidh na croitearachd, gu robh na h-aingil air nèamh agus spioradan an sinnsirean a' dèanamh iolaich, agus gu robh na Gaidheil a-nis a' tòiseachadh a' tuigsinn an toirbheartas a dh'ullaich an Athair air nèamh dhaibh nan cuireadh iad gu buil gach dòigh a bha fon comhair gus fhaotainn.

Dh'fhuirich còrr is ceud duine anns a' champa oidhche Dhimàirt, agus b' e siud an sealladh. Bha an oidhche brèagha da-rìreabh — oidhche rionnagach reòite gun sgòth air an adhar, is corran math gealaich ann. Bha Mòr Monadh agus Sìthean an Airgid air an dara taobh agus Loch Sìphort mu an coinneamh is e cho ciùin ri gloinne. Bha cabraichean agus siùil ann an cumadh an litir 'L' a' cumail glaodh an reothaidh a-muigh agus còig teinntean mòra a' toirt blàiths agus solais dhaibh anns a' phàillean fhosgailte anns an robh iad a' cur seachad na h-oidhche.

Air madainn Dimàirt thainig dithis fhir-naidheachd à Steòrnabhagh, Seumas Mac A' Phearsain agus Iain MacCoinnich, a-nall a Bhail' Ailean agus chaidh iad a-mach don Phàirc feuch am faiceadh iad dè a bha a' dol.

Nuair a thill an dithis a Bhail' Ailean mu chòig uairean feasgar Dimàirt agus gun iad air mòran fhaicinn fhad 's a bha iad anns an fhrìth — oir cha robh iad eòlach air monadh — cho-èignich iad am maighstir-sgoile, gus an toirt anmoch oidhche Dhimàirt chun a' champa ri taobh Loch Sìphort.

Nuair a bha iad mu choinneamh Airigh Dhòmhnaill Chaim, far an robh an campa, dh'èigh na croitearan cò iad, agus nuair a fhreagair Dòmhnall MacRath fhuair iad fàilte agus furan, agus chaidh iad air tìr. Bha an luchd-campachaidh an sin, cuid a' conaltradh is cuid a' gabhail òran, nam measg òran Mhic An t-Saoir, 'Chunna mi 'n damh donn 's na h-èildean.'

Dh'innis iad do mhuinntir Steòrnabhaigh gur h-e an èiginn is an t-acras a thug orra a dhol air 'Reud na Pàirce'. Anns a' champa an oidhche sin chaidh an Leabhar a ghabhail agus dh'fheuch cuid norrag cadail fhaighinn.

Air madainn Diciadain chaidh falbh ro bhriseadh an latha agus mar a bha an latha a' dol seachad bha tuilleadh is tuilleadh dhaoine a' dèanamh air a' Phàirc gus mu dheireadh gu robh barrachd a-muigh na bha muigh Dimàirt. Chan eil fhios cia mheud fiadh a chaidh a mharbhadh — bha cuid de na croitearan a' meas gun leagadh timcheall air ceithir cheud, ach bha Mgr Branckner aig an robh Ath Linne aig an àm ag radh ri luchd nam pàipearan naidheachd nach deach a mharbhadh ach dà fhiadh. Saoilidh mi gur h-e mu dhà cheud fiadh an àireamh bu choltaiche.

Air feasgar Diciadain nuair a bha Riaghladair nam Maor Sìth (Superintendent) Seumas Gòrdan agus an Siorraidh Friseal anns a' Phàirc, choinnich iad ri còmhlan de chroitearan aig an Ruadh Chleit faisg air Brollum. Dh'iarr an Siorraidh orra sgapadh agus dèanamh air an taighean ach dhiùlt iadsan sin a dhèanamh. An sin leugh an Siorraidh *Achd na h-Aimhreite* agus mhìnich e do na croitearan dè a bha i a' ciallachadh. Dh'innis iadsan dhà-san dè a thug orra an lagh a bhriseadh agus a dhol air tòir nam fiadh — agus b' e an t-adhbhar air sin an cruaidh-chàs agus a' bhochdainn a bha iad a' fulang. Dh'èisd an Siorraidh riutha gu furachail agus dh'fhalbh na daoine an uair sin dhachaigh.

Dh'atharraich an t-sìde Diardaoin agus rinn a' chuid mhòr de na daoine air an taigh, ach dh'fhuirich buidheann an siud 's an seo ri sealg. Co-dhiù bha dìth pheilearan orra, oir tha e coltach nach robh peilear ri fhaotainn ann an Steòrnabhagh.

Bha nis an sgeul air a dhol fada is farsaing agus ged a bha a' chuid mhòr de phàipearan-naidheachd na rìoghachd air taobh nan croitearan, bha cuid eile mar an *Scotsman* ag ràdh gu robh làn thìde muinntir nan Loch a chur sìos le làmhachas-làidir agus an toirt fo bhinn an lagha. Sin dìreach an rud a bha ann an rùn an Riaghaltais agus chuir iad 80 saighdear gu ruige Steòrnabhagh agus dh'òrdaich iad an long-chogaidh *Ajax* seòladh à Grianaig agus dèanamh air Steòrnabhagh.

Air madainn Disathairn, an siathamh latha fichead den t-Samhain, thàinig am maor-sìth Sgt Mac A' Ghobhainn à Steòrnabhagh gu taigh-sgoile Bhail' Ailein agus dh'fhaighnich e do Dhòmhnall MacRath an robh e an dùil an toireadh na creachadairean iad fhèin suas no am feumadh an Riaghaltas làmhachas-làidir a chleachdadh. Thuirt am maighstir-sgoile ris gun toireadh iad iad fhèin suas, nan deigheadh iarraidh orra. Mar sin 's e cosgais gun fheum a bha ann a dhol a thoirt an airm agus long-chogaidh a Leòdhas idir — is iomadh diathad a dh'fhaodadh muinntir nan Loch a bhith air fhaighinn leis an airgead a chaidh a chosg. An uair a fhuair Sgt Mac A' Ghobhainn an gealltanas a bha seo on mhaighstir-sgoile rinn e air taobh deas an Loch, oir bhathas an tòir air ceithir duine deug de na cinn-feadhna ged is e seisear a chaidh a thoirt gu cùirt.

B' iad sin Dòmhnall MacRath, am maighstir-sgoile, Ruairidh Sheòrais agus Murchadh an Tàillear, an dithis à Bail'Ailean, Seonaidh an Mhurchaidh à Grabhair, Calum Alasdair Ruaidh agus Dòmhnall Aonghais Iain, an dithis à Crosbost.

B' iad fianaisean a' chrùin;

1	Ruairidh Mac a' Ghobhainn (Ruairidh Ruadh)
2	Murchadh Màrtainn
3	Calum Mac a' Ghobhainn (Calum Ruairidh Ruaidh)
4	Dòmhnall MacFhionghuin (Dòmhnall Thormoid) gu lèir à Bail'Ailean
5	Seumas Seòras Mac a' Phearsain (ceannaiche à Steòrnabhagh)
6	Iain MacCoinnich (Fear-Ionaid à Steòrnabhagh)
7	Dòmhnall MacLeòid (Dòmhnall Buachaill)
8	Iain Mac a' Ghobhainn (Iain Iain Ruaidh)
9	Calum Ceanadach (an triùir à Bail'Ailean)
10	Murchadh MacRath (geamair Isginn)
11	Fearchar MacRath (geamair Cheann-na-Caradh)
12	Coinneach MacMhaoilein (Coinneach Dhonnchaidh)
13	Iain Ceanadach (an dithis à Leumrabhagh)
14	Seumas Gordon (Riaghladair nam Maor-sìth an Steòrnabhagh)

Chruinnich còrr air mìle neach ann an Steòrnabhagh an oidhche a bha na seisear a' seòladh chun na cùirt ann an Dùn Eideann, a' guidhe gun deigheadh gu math leotha. Thòisich a' chùirt madainn Diluain agus lean i fad an latha; 's ann aig dà mhionaid an dèidh ceithir feasgar Dimàirt a chaidh a' bhinn a thoirt a-mach. B' e a' bhinn gun robh an seisear neo-chiontach de na chaidh a chur às an leth. Bha àrd-iolach air sràidean Dhùn Eidinn am feasgar ud. Chaidh Dòmhnall MacRath a ghiùlan air guaillibh a chàirdean is am mòr-shluagh a' dèanamh luathghaire is gàirdeachais; agus an ath latha fhuair iad fàilte is furan bho mhuinntir Ghlaschu cuideachd. Chaidh coinneamh a chumail ann an Seòmraichean *Waterloo* agus rinn Dòmhnall MacRath òraid a bha ainmeil.

Bha fear-lagha comasach, Mac Gille Sheathaich, a' dìon MhicRath agus nan croitearan

A' bhean-uasal Seasaidh Platt.

aig a' chùirt ann an Dùn Eideann agus 's e a' chasaid a bha nan aghaidh gu robh iad a' dèanamh tuaireap agus àimhreit anns a' Phàirc.

Dh'fhaighnich am fear-lagha den chùirt, "Cionnas a bha àimhreit ann ma bha Mgr Thorneycroft, am bràthair a b' òige aig a' Bhean-uasal Platt a' roinn a chuid bìdh is dibhe am measg nan croitearan?"

Bha Donnchadh Mòr, nach maireann, mac Mhurchaidh Mhòir, an t-àrd gheamair aig an àm, den bheachd gur e an coibhneas agus a' bhàidhealachd a thug Mgr. Thorneycroft do na croitearan a chaidh a thoirt gu cùirt, a shàbhail iad, agus dh'fhaodadh sin a bhith ceart.

Cha tug Mgr. Dòmhnall MacRath fada ann am Bail' Ailean an dèidh siud. Dh'fhàg e anns an Earrach 1889, agus dh'fhàg e cuimhneachain mhath na dhèidh.

Seo an rud mu dheireadh a sgrìobh e ann an Leabhar Eachdraidh na sgoile:

"Dh'fhosgail mi an sgoil an diugh airson na h-uair mu dheireadh. Bhruidhinn mi ris a' chloinn aig uair feasgar agus dh'earalaich mi iad a bhith fìrinneach agus onarach agus dìcheallach nan dreuchd; urram a thoirt do dhuine sam bith, ge b' e cò e, nan dleasadh a chaithe-beatha urram; iad strì ri deagh-ghean gach duine chosnadh agus gun eagal neach no nì a bhith orra ach a-mhàin eagal ron olc. Le sin ghuidh mi beannachd leotha."

9 Aimhreit Aignis 1888

Iain MacArtair

Chan eil duine beò an-diugh a ghabh compàirt anns an iorghail a bha an Aignis san Rubha an Leòdhas aig deireadh na naoidheamh linne deug. Chaochail am fear mu dheireadh aca, de na prìosanaich, o chionn dhà no trì bhliadhnachan — Iain MacAoidh à Aignis (Càbhais), bràthair mo sheanar. Chan eil ach fìor chorra fhear anns an sgìre aig a bheil càil ach fiar chuimhne air an latha ud air am bi luaidh fhada ann an eachdraidh an eilein, an uair a theab cinn a bhith air am briseadh is fuil a bhith air a dòirteadh. Chan fhaighear mar sin an-diugh cunntas mionaideach bho bheul-aithris air a' chùis, mar a chaidh a sgrìobhadh le fear Seumas Camshron, a bha na fhear-fhianais air na thachair an latha ud; ach tha, fhathast, corra sgeul ri fhaotainn bho bheul-aithris an t-sluaigh, agus ann an aon thachartas air a bheil an Camshronach a' luaidh, chì sinn nach do thog e ceart dè a chaidh a ràdh.

Aig Sealbh tha brath dè a dh'adhbhraich an aimhreit an latha ud; chan eil duine ro chinnteach, ach saoilidh mi, a deidh a bhith ann an còmhradh nam bodach, is bho bheul-aithris, nach b' e aon rud na dà rud a b'adhbhar don èirigh a chaidh a dhèanamh. Bha a' Ghàidhealtachd gu lèir air bhoil aig aon àm le aintighearnas nan uachdaran, is bha cuimhne ro ghoirt aig na bha air am fàgail air fògradh an athraichean. Bha barrachd spèis do chrodh is do chaoraich na do bheatha duine. Cha robh seilbh sam bith aca air an fhearann a bha iad ag àiteachadh, is bha am màl fada seachad air na b' fhiach na feannagan bochda aca. Mar shàmhla air làmhachas-làidir an ama sin tha an sgeul seo againn air an t-Siamarlan Rothach, am fear-millidh a chuir Leòdhas bun os cionn. Bha e togail a' mhàil am Pabail, is thurchair gun robh aon de na croitearan a bha an sin, Calum Fhionnlaigh, le car na bheul bhon bhroinn. Shaoil leis an Rothach gur e diombadh a bha air ris fhèin. "Tasdan airson do ghreann" ars esan, "air neo bidh mach às do thaigh gun dàil." Bha an Rothach cuideachd aig an àm seo air òrdugh a thoirt seachad nach fhaodadh mac màthar san Rubha pòsadh mur a biodh fearann aige gun tugadh e a bhean. Dè an t-iongnadh a rèisde ged a leanadh mallachd an t-sluaigh an Rothach chun na crìche is ged nach tugadh iad urram a bhàis fhèin dha. 'S e theireadh na croitearan, a' dùnadh na h-uaghach aige, "Cuiribh air, cuiribh air; chuireadh e fhèin oirnne." Bha cuideachd èirigh na Pàirce, far na chreach muinntir nan Loch frìthean na mnatha uasail Platt, air los bidhe don teaghlaichean, ùr ann an cuimhne an t-sluaigh is thug iad an aire gun sheall muinntir nam bailtean mòra mòran co-fhaireachdainn ri muinntir nan Loch aig àm na cùirte aca, is an dèidh an leigeil fo sgaoil. Bha fir an Rubha geur-chùiseach gu leòr gus faicinn gun robh sùilean na rìoghachd air bochdainn an eilein, is gum b' e seo an t-àm iomchaidh nan robh iad a' dol a sheasamh airson an còirichean, agus bha bochdainn anns an eilean gun teagamh, ach cha chreid mi gun robh a' ghort a riamh ann, cho fad 's a bhiodh iasg an cuan, maorach air cladach, mult air sliabh is bò air stèill.

Chuir a h-uile càil a bha sin boil air muinntir an Rubha is thàinig a' chùis gu aona-cheann. Cha robh iad gu bhith bliadhna eile gun cheartas a thagradh, air an sgàth fhèin agus air sgàth an cuid chloinne. B' e Mac Alasdair aig an robh taca Aignis aig an àm a dhìol air a seo, oir bha esan mar shamhla dhaibh air an ùghdarras a bha gan sàrachadh. Chuir iad an comhairle ri chèile is chaidh fios a chur gu bàillidh an fhearainn an Steòrnabhagh gu robh iad a' dol a sgiùrsadh sprèidh MhicAlasdair aig uair àraid, air a leithid seo a latha. Bha fìor fhios aig an Rothach nach b' ann ri fealla-dhà a bha na seòid is leig e ris do na maoir-sìthe an lideadh a fhuair e. Bha buidheann shaighdearan de na *Royal Scots,* fo iùil Chaiptein MhicFhearchair stèidhichte ann an Steòrnabhagh air tàille ar-a-mach den t-seòrsa seo, is fhuair an caiptean fios dèanamh air Mealabost cho fàthach is a thigeadh aige air, gu bhith ann mun tigeadh na daoine. Dh'fhalbh na saighdearan am marbhan na h-oidhche is chaidh iad air fiaradh na machrach gus na ràinig iad an ceann-uidhe is chaidh an cumail an sin, gun fhios nach deigheadh aig na croitearan air an sprèidh a ruagadh cho fada ri sin. Aig lethuair an deidh sia air madainn bhreagha, thàinig fir às a' chabhlaich rìoghail, fo stiùireadh Chaiptean Plumbe, air tìr aig beul an Loch a Tuath is shnàig iad a null beul na mara is tarsainn nan dùn gainmheach gus na gheàrr iad thairis aig seann chladh na h-Aoidhe, is an sin chaidh iad am falach an saibhlean na tuatha. Eadar a seachd 's a h-ochd, thàinig ochd maoir-sìthe às a' bhaile, is aig briseadh na fàire, nochd an Siorram Friseal is Iain Rois, fear-tagraidh a' chrùin, aig taigh na taca. Bha gach nì a nis an òrdugh gu coinneachadh a dhèanamh ris na bheireadh a' mhadainn mun cuairt.

Bha an seachdamh latha den Fhaoilleach, ochd ceud deug, ceithir fichead 's a h-ochd, a rèir eachdraidh, na latha eadar dhà shian. Aig deich uairean sa mhadainn, bha mu chòig ceud duine, eadar fir is mnathan, cruinn air leathad a' chnuic os cionn na taca. Bha caman aig grunn aca nan làimh is aig cuid eile clachan a bha iad air a thogail bhon talamh anns an dol seachad. Bha an fhìor chuthach orra ach bu bhochd an armachd seo gu dhol an coinneimh luaidhe is stàillinn nan saighdearan, nan tigeadh orra sin a dhèanamh. Tha an Gàidheal mall gu feirg, ach bha iad seo air an cur thuige le aintighearnas, ann an dòigh 's gur e mìorbhail nam mìorbhailean nach deach fuil a dhòirteadh. Cha robh an Siorram Friseal idir gun làn bheachd aige air an seo; bu Ghàidheal e fhèin is tha iomadh rann molaidh air gus an latha an-diugh. Chan eil teagamh sam bith, mar tha an Camshronach ag radh, nach robh am meas a bha aig an t-sluagh air, mar dhuine fìor agus ceart, mar mheadhan air sìth a chur air an aisith. Bha crith na làimh agus tuar air aodann an là ud nach robh bhon aois a-mhàin ged a bha e air a thighinn gu latha mòr.

Cho luath 's a ghluais na croitearan, thug e fhèin is Iain Rois ceum abhsaidh nan

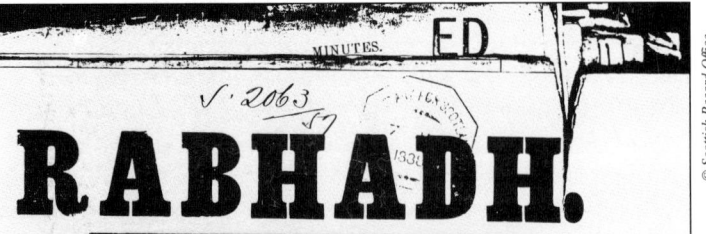

RABHADH.

A CHIONN 's gun d' fhuair an Luchd-ughdarrais fios gu 'm bheil Comhchruinneachadh sluaigh, an uine ghoirid, gu oidhirp mi-laghail a thoirt air an stoc fhuadach dheth Gabhail-fearainn Aignis, ann an Sgireachd Steornabha, agus sealbh a ghabhail air an fhearann: tha so a toirt Rabhadh gu 'm bheil cruinneachadh sluaigh air son an aobhar sin no aobhar sam bith eile dhe leithid mi-laghail agus ciontach, agus gu 'm bi na h-uil*i* neach a ghabhas pairt ann, ged theagamh nach dean gach neach air leth foirneart, ciontach de bhi togail buaireas agus aimhreite, agus gu 'm bi iad buailteach do pheanas. Agus a thuilleadh air sin tha so a toirt Rabhadh gu 'm bheil cruinneachidhean de 'n ghne ud air an toirmeasg; agus ma ni sluagh aimhreiteach mi-riaghailteach cruinneachadh gu'n teid, a reir an "RIOT ACT," GLAODHAICH mar so a dheanamh:— "Tha ar n-ARD-BHAINTIGH-"EARNA, a' BHAN-RIGH a toirt aithne agus ordugh do 'n "t-sluagh a tha cruinn sgaoileadh gu h-ealamh, agus falbh gu "siochail a dhionnsuidh an dachaighean no chun an gnothuichean "laghail, air neo gum bi iad buailteach do na peanasan a tha air "an ainmeachadh anns an Reachd a chaidh dheanamh an "ciad bhliadhna Righ Sheorais, a chum bacadh a chuir air "iorghuillean agus cruinneachidhean aimhreiteach." "Gu'n "gleidheadh Dia a' Bhan-righ;" agus mar sgaoil cruinneachadh 'sam bith de 'n ghne ud, an taobh a stigh de dh' uair an deigh na Glaodhaich ud, bithidh gach neach a bhitheas ann ciontach de 'n chionta ud, agus buailteach do na peanasan cruaidh tha an Reachd ud ag ordachadh.

LE ORDUGH AN T-SIORRA.

TEARLACH INNES,

Inbhirfeotharan, 2mh January, 1888.   Cleireach-Siorra Siorramachd Rois.

Achd na h-Aimhreite a chaidh a leughadh dha fir Aignis.

coinneimh is thug e earal dhaibh mu na cunnartan anns an robh iad gan cur fhèin is an teaghlaichean, is dh'àithn e dhaibh, san Ghàidhlig, iad a thilleadh dhachaigh, ach cha tugadh na seòid feart air, is thòisich iad a' trusadh an sprèidh. Chaidh na saighdearan is na maoir-sìthe nam bad is bha sabaid chruaidh ann a lean còrr is lethuair a-thìde.

Faodaidh beachd a bhith againn air an othail is an ùpraid le èigheachd nam ban, mèilich chaorach, is nuallaich cruidh, is fuaim nam buillean. Chaidh aig an t-sluagh air an sprèidh a thrusadh romhpa ach chaill iad an t-sabaid is chaidh duine no dhithis aca a chur an sàs. Bha fìor bheachd aig na maoir cò na ceannardan a bha orra (leithid Corodaidh is an Goistidh às an Aird) is rinn iad ionnsaigh air an cur-san fo cheannsal co-dhiù, ach fhuair fear no dhà dhiubh às. Leum Iain Ruairidh Bhàin dìg mhòr an Uillt Dhuibh is i na leum ach cha leumadh duine a bha às a dhèidh i. Thàrr esan às. Chaidh Cailean Fhionnlaigh a ghlacadh air a bruaich.

Bha an sluagh a-nis aig oisean a' Ghàrraidh Ghil — àite cumhang eadar dà ghàrradh àrd aig ceann a' Bhràighe. Their iad chun an latha an-diugh gum faodadh iad a bhith air na saighdearan a chur fodha an seo, nam b' e an toil e, 's gun chothrom tionndaidh aca. Seo far na theab an call a bhith. Thug an sluagh ionnsaigh chruaidh air na prìosanaich thoirt bho na maoir, is tharraing Iain Rois an daga aige. Chuir seo an tuilleadh corraich orra. Leum iad air is dh'èigh fear aca, nan deigheadh peilear a losgadh gun cuireadh iad na saighdearan dhachaigh lomnochd. Tharraing na saighdearan na biodagan ach choisich na seòid thuca gus an robh an stàillinn rim broillichean. Leugh an siorram *Achd na h-Aimhreite* am Beurla is an Gàidhlig is ghuidh e gu dùrachdach orra sgur air sgàth Nì Math. Cha robh fios dè a bha dol a thachairt ach rùisg 'Caiptean' MhicPhàil a bhroilleach, is thuirt e ris an t-saighdear a b' fhaisge, 'Sàth an siud do bhiodag!' An uair a dhiùlt e, dh'èigh an 'caiptean' ris na saighdearan, 'Falbhaibh is marbhaibh na cearcan; chan eil an còrr a dh'fheum annaibh!' Thog an Camshronach seo ceàrr. Co-dhiù chòrd a' bharail a bh' aig a' Chaiptean air na saighdearan, ris an t-sluagh. Rinn iad lachan gàire is cha deach a' chùis na bu mhiosa.

Chaidh fios a chur a-nis air na saighdearan a bha feitheamh am Mealabost gu cuideachadh chàich, ach a dh'aindeoin an còmhnadh a rinn iadsan dhaibh, 's ann air fìor èiginn a chaidh na prìosanaich a chur an làimh is an toirt air falbh. Anns an iorghal ùir seo chaidh an tuilleadh a ghlacadh, aon aca co-dhiù aig nach robh cuid no gnothach ris na thachair. B' e seo Iain MacAoidh air an tug mi iomradh an toiseach, an t-aon a b' òige aca. Bha e na ghille òg a' dol a dh'iarraidh biadhadh maoraich don tràigh is chaidh e shealltainn dè mar a bha a' dol dhaibh. 'S e bun a bha ann gun robh e air àireamh nam prìosanach, aon duine deug aca, a chaidh fhiachainn an Dùn Eideann agus a fhuair bliadhna de phrìosan an duine. Bha duine no dithis eile a chaidh an cur an sàs, ged is beag a shaoil iad a thachradh sin an uair a dh'èirich iad anns a' mhadainn. Bha Ailean a' Phìobaire à Beinn na Saighde air ùr thighinn

Ailean Dòmhnallach à Beinn na Saighde, fear de phrìosanaich Aignis.

dhachaigh bho sheòladh is gu mì-shealbhach siud an latha a chuir e roimhe a dhol a shealltainn air cuideachd a mhàthar ann am Pabail. Gus slighe ghoirid a dhèanamh dheth, gheàrr e tarsainn na machrach is ràinig e Aignis an uair bu teotha a bha an t-sabaid. Bha e òg treun is cha robh càil a b' fheàrr na dhol a-steach na mheadhan agus is e bun a bha ann gun deach a chur an grèim.

Bha Dòmhnall Macleòid, 'Am Boer', à Seiseadar air a shlighe dhachaigh à Steòrnabhagh le ìocshlaint dha mhàthair, is i tinn, is cha do ràinig e fhèin no a adhbharturais dhachaigh an oidhche sin.

Dh'fhalbh na saighdearan leis na prìosanaich suas don bhaile is chaidh an cur fo ghlais- Cailean Fhionnlaigh is Murchadh Anndra à Pabail; Calum mac Alasdair Mhòir; Uilleam mac Thormoid agus Iain a mhac; Iain 'ic Iain; Murchadh Ruairidh; Dòmhnall mac Dhòmhnaill, uile às an Aird; Iain Mhurchaidh Nèill bhon Chnoc is Ailean a' Phìobaire a' Beinn a Saighde. Bha iad gealtach is treun an latha ud a rèir òran tè Phabail:

'S mis' tha fo mhì-run,is mis' tha fo bhròn
Mo smuain air do leannan a muigh aig a' mhòd.
Dh'aithnichinn mo leannan a' siubhal an rathaid
Le bhrògan tana is 'lastic' nam beòil.
Chaluim Dhòmhnaill ic Dhonnchaidh is mairg dhèanadh earbs' asd-
An uair a rug iad air Murchadh, dh' fhalbh sibhs' mar na h-eòin.

Cha deach an cumail a-staigh an Steòrnabhagh ach an aon oidhche is fhuair iad cead an coise an latharna-mhàireach gun tigeadh àm na cùirte aca, ach bha iad fo bhòidean nach fhàgadh iad an t-eilean is bha sùil nam maor orra a h-uile ceum. Ged a chaidh an gairm an Steòrnabhagh is e Ard-chùirt Dhùin Eideinn a bha ri am fiachainn is am binn a thoirt a-mach. Bha an Siorram Friseal agus am fear-tagraidh an Steòrnabhagh air a bhith nan sùil-fhianais air na thachair an latha ud. Thug na cùisean seo mìos no dhà mun deach an stèidheachadh agus bha toiseach an t-samhraidh ann mun tàinig latha na cùirte aca.

Air madainn àlainn san Ghiblein, dh'èirich muinntir Phabail gu sealladh neo-àbhaisteach. Bha soitheach-cogaidh, an *Sea-Horse*, air acair air a' bhàgh le còmhlan shaighdearan air bòrd. Dh'aithnich iad anns a' bhad nach b' ann bhon fhèath a bha an uspag, is chaidh iad air an casan. Ro mheadhan latha chunnacas buidheann mhaor-sithe steach an rathad is dh'aithnich iad an uair sin le cinnt gur ann air tòir nam prìosanach a bha iad. Nan èireadh fir a' bhaile is ann a bhiodh a' chùis na bu mhiosa is an tuilleadh trioblaid ann, ach cha robh na mnathan aca idir a' dol a ghèilleadh cho furasda. Nam falbhadh na fir, dh'fhalbhadh an cosnadh agus is ann air na mnathan a thuiteadh uallach taighe is cloinne is cha bu bheag e anns na laithean a rug orra. Chruinnich iad às gach ceàrn den bhaile, iarach is uarach, Geilir,

Murchadh Dòmhnallach (clì gu h-ìseal), 6 An Aird, fear de na prìosanaich.

Iain MacAoidh agus a mhac Iain. B' e Iain (a bu shine) an t-aon phrìosanach a fhuair croit nuair a bhriseadh Aignis an 1905.

*Dòmhnall MacLeòid
1 Seisiadar, An Rubha.*

A' Phàirc, An Creagan, An Tobhta Raineach is Clèid is chaidh iad gun gheilt an coinneimh nam maor. Ghabh iad do na maoir leis na clachan is leis na fàdan is chuir iad an ruaig gu tur orra air ais a Steòrnabhagh. 'S e balach math a chumadh aghaidh ri trì cheud boireannach is an dearg chuthach orra!

Cha robh air, a nis, ach feitheamh feuch dè bheireadh an uair mun cuairt is cha robh fada aca ri feitheamh. Chunnacas na saighdearan a' tighinn air tìr air an Sgaoilteach is a' dèanamh air na taighean. Tha iad fhathast ann a chunnaic an sealladh ud, is rinn e uidhir a dhrùidheadh orra is nach do chaill iad cuimhne a riamh air. Cha robh Màiri a' Phreasaich ach na trì bliadhna, ach chì i fhathast lainnir nam beuglaid ris a' ghrèin mar gum b' ann an dè a bhiodh e.

Chaidh na saighdearan gu na taighean is rug iad air Cailean Fhionnlaigh is chaidh Murchadh Anndra a thoirt à leabaidh tinneis is a chur an grèim. Their beul-aithris fhathast nach robh leithid a fhrithealadh orra nam beatha 's a bha orra am prìosan Chaltoin an Dùn Eideann. Bha am biadh cinnteach dhaibh co-dhiù. Bha iad air ais nan dachaighean an ceann sia mìosan.

Is math dh'fhaoidte nach robh mòran èifeachd aig an àm anns na rinn iad air an latha iomraideach seo ach thug iad aire a' mhòr-shluaigh às ùr gu suidheachadh bochd an eilein, is gu an crannchur, is rinn iad oidhirp air an saorsa is an còirichean dligheach a ghlacadh. Bu bhuaidh sin fhèin. Rinn iadsan am measradh, ach b' e na h-àil a lean iad a bhlais air an ìm.

10 Col Uarach agus Griais

Seòras Stiùbhart

Seo an eachdraidh as aosmhor a tha againn mu Thac Ghriais. Bha i air a h-àiteachadh aig Murchadh Moireasdan aig toiseach an t-seachdamh linn deug; agus bha e pòsta aig piuthar Dhòmhnaill Chaim à Uig.

Tha e coltach gu robh na Moireasdanaich agus Clann 'Ic Amhlaidh air sìth a dhèanamh ri chèile aig an àm seo.

Bha Murchadh air ainmeachadh mar Mac Mhic Ailein Mhic a' Bhreitheimh. Anns an linn seo bha Clann Mhic Coinnich air tighinn a riaghladh an eilein agus cha robh taobh aca ris na Moireasdanaich agus chuir iad Iain Mac Mhurchaidh air falbh bhon Tac agus chaidh a chur gu Tac Chuil Uaraich. Cha robh an Tac seo cho mòr ri Tac Ghriais agus a rèir eachdraidh cha tug e ach ùine ghoirid ann an sin. Thog sluagh Chuil droch innleachdan na aghaidh agus chaidh e a-null a Bhràgair. Tha e coltach gur h-e duine foghlaimte a bh' ann an Iain agus dh'fhàg e mòran eachdraidh mu dheidhinn an Eilein.

Beagan ùine an dèidh seo, dh'èirich argamaid ann an Col Uarach mu chrìochan a' bhaile agus thàinig Iain a nall à Bràgair a dhèanamh rèite.

Seo mar a dh'ainmich e a' chrìoch:

"Tha chrìoch am bùth nan naosg
'S ma tharraingeas tu an taod teann
Dhan bhota dhomhainn seo shuas
'S e sin Col Uarach nam beann."

Bha fhios aig Iain nach robh duine aca a leughadh no a sgrìobhadh agus 's e seo dòigh air an glèidheadh iad a' chùis nan cuimhne.

Aig toiseach an ochdamh linn deug, thug Clann 'Ic Coinnich Clann 'Ic Iomhair don eilean agus shuidhich iad fear ann an Griais agus beagan ùine an dèidh sin shuidhich iad fear eile ann an Col Uarach. Aig toiseach an naodhamh linn deug bha Lewis MacIomhair na uachdaran air Tac Ghriais agus Cailean MacIomhair ann an Col Uarach.

Bha mòran dhaoine a' còmhnaidh air iomall nan tac agus bha iad fo smachd an uachdarain agus a thuilleadh air pàigheadh màil airson am beagan fearainn a bha aca, dh'fheumadh iad mòran obrach a dhèanamh dhan uachdaran.

Bha cùisean cruadalach aig an àm seo agus a thuilleadh air na bha tachairt, bha cùisean na bu mhiosa a' feitheamh orra.

Bheachdaich na h-uachdarain gun co-èignicheadh iad na daoine air falbh bho na feannagan talmhainn a bha aca agus gun cuireadh iad caoraich mhaola nan àite. Bha cuid aca a chaidh thairis air chuan agus cuid eile a fhuair croitean air a' Bhac agus ann an Col ach cha robh grèim laghail aca air na croitean aig an àm sin.

Nuair a chaochail Lewis MacIomhair ann an 1845, 's e a mhac Seumas a chaidh na àite ann an Griais ach cha robh cùisean a' dol leis agus fhuair fear Pàdraig Liddle an tac agus na dhèidh-san fhuair mac a bhràthar sealbh air.

Nuair a dh'fhàg Cailean MacIomhair Col Uarach agus a chaidh e a dh'Aimearaga thàinig fear Ruairidh MacNeacail na àite agus nuair a dh'fhalbh esan 's e fear Iain Mac an t-Sealgair a fhuair sealbh air agus na dhèidh-san fhuair a mhac Teàrlach e.

'S e seo na tuathanaich a bha làthair nuair a thàinig an t-Achd a-mach ann an 1912 a' rùnachadh na tuathan a roinn nan croitean. Chuir an Cogadh Mòr dàil air a' chùis agus mun do sguir an cogadh, bha am Morair Lever air an Eilean a cheannach agus bha e na rùn na tuathan a ghlèidheadh teàrainte agus bha e faicsinneach nach b' e caraid a' chroiteir a bh' ann.

Nuair a thill mòran dhaoine às a' Chogadh Mhòr agus cuid aca gun thaigh gun fhearann agus air dhaibh a thuigsinn gun robh an t-Achd agus na geallaidhean gu bhith air am briseadh agus cruadal an athraichean a' co-fhreagairt ris an dòigh-beatha a bhiodh aca fo ùghdaras a' Mhorair Lever, chuir iad an comhairle ri chèile agus dh'aontaich iad gun tugadh iad dùbhlan do Lever.

Thog iad bothanan air Tac Ghriais agus Chuil Uaraich agus thòisich gach fear aca air àiteach mìrean de thalamh.

Mòchan, a' chiad ghaisgeach a fhuair taigh air an t-seann tuathanas.

Lean an aimhreit a' dol mu dhà bhliadhna agus mu dheireadh b'èiginn do Lever strìochdadh dhaibh agus chaidh na tacan a roinn nan croitean.

Bha na seòid air ceithir bliadhna a chur seachad anns a' Chogadh ri aghaidh teine agus mòran chunnartan.

Mar a thuirt iad fhèin, cha robh Bodach Beag an t-Siabainn a' dol a chur geilt orra-san.

Seo a-nis beagan eachdraidh mu na rudan a chunnaic mi aig àm an aimhreit ann an Griais, mar a thog iad bothanan agus a thòisich iad air àiteachadh mìrean den tac.

Thuirt Bòrd an Fhearainn ris na daoine a bha còmhnaidh anns na bothanan nach biodh e furasta an talamh a roinn na chroitean agus iad fuireach air an talamh.

Rinn na daoine an rud a chaidh iarraidh orra agus dh'fhàg iad na bothanan ach bha ceithir "raiders" le an teaghlaichean gun àite aca anns am fuiricheadh iad agus cho-èignich iad Bòrd an Fhearainn gu feumadh iad ionadan còmhnaidh a thoirt dhaibh fhad 's a bhiodh iad a' roinn an fhearainn.

Iain Mac An t-Sealgair le cuid de theaghlach aig Taigh Mòr Chuil c 1906-10.

Dh'èisd am Bòrd ris a' chùis-thagraidh sin agus thog iad ceithir taighean sinc dhaibh air taobh a' Bhac de Abhainn Ghriais. Seo a nis ainmean nam fear a fhuair na taighean sin:

    Murchadh Greumach   (mac Alasdair Mhic Dhòmhnaill bho 8 am Bac)
    Dòmhnall Mac Illeathain   (mac Iain Dhòmhnaill bho 6 am Bac)
    Ailean Màrtainn   (mac Thormoid Buachaill bho 59 am B ac)
    Ruairidh MacLeòid   (mac Dhòmhnaill Aonghais bho 44 am Bac)

Thug iad beagan ùine a' tàmh anns na taighean sin agus nuair a chaidh gnothaichean a rèiteachadh ann an Griais chaidh iad gu na croitean a bha air an cur a-mach dhaibh, agus thug gach fear a thaigh leis.

Chaidh taigh an tac agus mu shia acair fearainn agus a' mhuileann bhleith fhàgail aig Pàdraig Liddle, fear an tac. A thuilleadh air an sin, chaidh an taigh agus beagan fearainn fhàgail aig a' gheamair.

Chuala sinn agus leugh sinn mu eachdraidh nam fuadaichean agus na rudan dona agus ciùrrail a dh'fhuiling an sluagh — an taighean gan cur nan teine agus gan ruagadh a thìrean cèin. 'S e Cloinn Ic Choinnich a bha a' riaghladh an eilein aig an àm a bha na nithean uabhasach sin a' tachairt agus chaidh fàisneachd a dhèanamh mu thimcheall nan oighrichean aca, gum biodh iad dall agus bacach 's air a' cheann mu dheireadh nach biodh oighre idir ann.

Tha e iongantach gu robh beagan den fhàisneachd seo fìrinneach mu thimcheall tac Ghriais oir cha d' fhuair duine leis an sloinneadh MacChoinnich croit ann an Griais.